Baby Boomers

AGEING IN THE 21ST CENTURY

Edited by
Maria Evandrou

© 1997 Maria Evandrou
Published by Age Concern England
1268 London Road
London SW16 4ER

First published 1997

Design and production Eugenie Dodd Typographics
Copy preparation Vinnette Marshall
Printed in Great Britain by Bell & Bain Ltd, Glasgow

A catalogue record for this book is available
from the British Library

ISBN 0–86242–153–5

CONTENTS

ABOUT THE AUTHORS

Gillian Dalley is Director of the Centre for Policy on Ageing. She is an anthropologist and her career has been predominantly in health services research. She is the author of *Ideologies of Caring: Rethinking community and collectivism*.

Maria Evandrou is a Fellow in Health Policy Analysis at the King's Fund Policy Institute, and Associate Research Fellow on the Welfare State Programme, London School of Economics. She is co-editor (with S Arber) of *Ageing, Independence and the Life Course*.

Jane Falkingham is a lecturer in Population Studies in the Department of Social Policy at the London School of Economics, and Research Fellow on the Welfare State Programme, also at the LSE. She is the co-author (with Paul Johnson) of *Ageing and Economic Welfare* and co-editor of *Social Security and Social Change: The dynamic of welfare* and, most recently, *Household Welfare in Central Asia*.

Ruth Hancock is an economist with a special interest in economic well-being in later life and the economics of ageing. She is Senior Research Fellow at the Age Concern Institute of Gerontology, and has co-authored several publications, including (with Claire Jarvis) *The Long-term Effects of being a Carer* and (with Claire Jarvis and Ganka Mueller) *The Outlook for Incomes in Retirement*.

Jane Lewis was Professor of Social Policy at the London School of Economics until 1996 and is now a Fellow of All Souls College, Oxford, and Director of the Wellcome Unit for the History of Medicine. She is the author of many books and articles on social policy, including, with Howard Glennerster, *Implementing the New Community Care; The voluntary sector, the state and social work in Britain* and, with Barbara Meredith, *Daughters Who Care*.

Robin Means is Reader in Social Gerontology at the School for Policy Studies, University of Bristol. He is co-author of *Community Care: Policy and practice* and co-editor of *Implementing Housing Policy*. He is currently working with colleagues on an inter-agency workbook for the Department of Health/Department of the Environment, entitled *Making Partnerships Work in Community Care: A guide for practitioners in housing, health and social services*.

Chris Phillipson is Professor of Applied Social Studies and Social Gerontology, and Director of the Centre for Social Gerontology, University of Keele. His research interests include social theory and ageing, social change and the family, and work and retirement. He has recently completed a large-scale study of kinship and old age in urban environments. He is the author of *Capitalism and the Construction of Old Age* and co-author of *The Sociology of Old Age*, of *Changing Work and Retirement* and of *Elder Abuse in Perspective*.

ACKNOWLEDGEMENTS

I would like to thank the various individuals who have contributed in different ways to the development of this book.

First, my gratitude goes to the six contributors for their co-operation, goodwill and patience.

In particular, I would like to acknowledge Evelyn McEwen's role in making it possible for me to consider putting such a publication together.

A number of people made time to read and comment on earlier drafts of the book, which was very helpful. My thanks go to Lorna Easterbrook, Evelyn McEwen, Louise Russell, Sally West and Jane Whelan. I am indebted to Jane Falkingham for her inspirational support.

Maria Evandrou
April 1997

INTRODUCTION

Maria Evandrou

Official government projections indicate that by 2026 the number of people aged 60 and over will reach 17.5 million (OPCS, 1995). This is an increase of nearly 50 per cent on the 11.9 million people in the same age category in 1991. Most of this increase is due to the retirement of the 'baby boomers' born in 1946–1950 or the early 1960s.

The large numbers approaching pensionable age, worsening dependency ratios and increased pressure on the social security budget has given rise to a growing literature on the social and economic costs of an ageing population (OECD, 1988; Johnson and Falkingham, 1992). Little attention, however, has been paid to the likely socio-economic characteristics of the baby boom generations in the first few decades of the twenty-first century, and how they may differ from previous groups of older people. Will universal membership of occupational and private pension schemes and greater home ownership mean that tomorrow's older population will be wealthier, no longer dependent on the state for income in retirement? Will they be healthier and fitter, making fewer demands on health and community services? Or will these 'children of the welfare state', with their better education and higher expectations, be more informed about their 'rights' and more vocal in their demands? What will be the role of information technology in their lives? What new calls will be placed on services, and the family, and how can and should policy makers begin to plan?

This book attempts to shed light on these questions. As we shall see in Chapter 1, Britain, unlike North America and Australia, has had two baby booms rather than one, and marked differences are to be expected between them and today's older people because they were born into and grew up in very different economic, technological and social climates. Table I.1 shows the age of people from different cohorts at selected social, economic and political events across the century. It is difficult to remember that people born in the peak birth year of 1964 were not even old enough to vote when Margaret Thatcher first came to power, yet Thatcherism and its legacy have shaped their experiences of adult life.

The differences between the experiences of people born before and after World War 2 is considerable, none of the latter having experienced large scale military conflict* and growing up under the umbrella of the welfare state, reaping the benefits of universal secondary education under the 1944 Education Act and expecting to receive health and social care 'from the cradle to the grave' under the National Health Service and the Social Services.

However, we should also be careful about treating both post-war baby boom cohorts as synonymous. The first baby boomers (1946–1950) were born in a period of post-war *austerity* – experiencing rationing and selective education. However, when they entered the labour market the economy was entering a period of relative *prosperity*. The job market was buoyant, and the rapid expansion of higher education in the 1960s meant that a growing number of them stayed on at school and entered university. In addition to new opportunities in education and work, the introduction of the contraceptive pill heralded a new sexual freedom. The spirit of the generation was captured in 1968 by the opening of the musical *Hair*, with its celebration of sex, drugs and nudity, whilst students protested in Grosvenor Square against the conflict in Vietnam and sit-ins were held at the London School of Economics and elsewhere.

In contrast, the second baby boomers (1961–65) were born into a period of *prosperity* – experiencing the consumer spending boom of the 1960s and comprehensive secondary education. But by the time they came to enter the labour market at the end of the 1970s, the economy was entering a recession, resulting in sharp rises in unemployment. People born during the peak birth year of 1964 reached school-leaving age in 1980 at the depth of recession. Some of this

---

* Although a minority these cohorts may have fought in the Falklands or Gulf War.

Table I.1 Age of selected birth cohorts at the time of political, economic and cultural events

EVENT	Birth cohort			
	1920	1935	1947	1964
1939 Hitler invades Poland	19	4		
1942 Publication of Beveridge Report	22	7		
1944 The Education Act establishes free secondary education as a universal right	24	9		
1945 World's first atom bomb (Hiroshima); end of World War 2	25	10		
1947 National Health Service launched	27	12	0	
1951 Korean War; 'Listen with Mother' launched	31	16	4	
1961 First man in space; Cold War deepens with Bay of Pigs stand-off and rise of the Berlin wall	41	26	14	
1963 Nelson Mandela jailed; JF Kennedy assassinated	43	28	16	
1965 Marines sent into Vietnam	45	30	18	1
1967 Homosexual acts between consenting adult males and abortion legalised; NHS makes contraception available on 'social grounds' (to married *and* unmarried women)	47	32	20	3
1971 Divorce Reform Act (1969) implemented	51	36	24	7
1973 Britain joins the Common Market	53	38	26	9
1974 Wilson elected (twice!); Nixon impeached; inflation tops 20%; comprehensive education introduced	54	39	27	10
1975 Equal Pay Act (1970) and Sex Discrimination Act implemented; SERPS established	55	40	28	11
1976 Britain goes 'cap in hand' to the International Monetary Fund	56	41	29	12
1979 Margaret Thatcher elected; Iran takes US hostages; USSR invades Afghanistan	59	44	32	15
1980 Housing Act introduces tenants' right to buy council homes	60	45	33	16
1982 Unemployment tops 3 million; War over Falklands	62	47	35	19
1985 Fowler social security review published, reforming SERPS; Live Aid	65	50	38	22

1987 Margaret Thatcher elected for 3rd term; Black Monday (Oct 19th)	67	52	40	23
1990 Mandela freed; riots over poll tax; invasion of Kuwait; Germany reunified; end of Thatcher era as Margaret resigns	70	55	43	26
1991 Communism ends and Soviet Union dismantled; GP fundholders and NHS trusts introduced	71	56	44	27
1993 Child Support Agency begins work; Jamie Bulger murdered; Maastricht treaty ratified	73	58	46	29
1995 Carers' needs recognised in Carers (Recognition and Services) Act 1995; Disability Discrimination Act 1995	75	60	48	31
1996 Job Seekers' Allowance comes into force; *Big Issue* celebrates 5th birthday	76	61	49	32
1997 Government White Paper *A New Partnership for Care in Old Age*	77	62	50	33

Source: Adapted from Evandrou and Falkingham (1997, Table 1).

group have *never* had a permanent full-time job. The spirit of radicalism and freedom, enjoyed by the preceding baby boom cohort, was missing – not only in terms of employment and income but also in other spheres of life. 1984 saw the first person diagnosed with AIDS, and so marked the end of the sexual revolution. In contrast to the 1960s, the 1980s were symbolised by the rise of the 'yuppy' (Young, Upwardly mobile Person) and the imperative of the private sector. Individualism rather than collectivism was the hallmark of the decade, the period witnessing an increasing polarisation of society and a widening gap between the 'haves' and the 'have nots' (Goodman and Webb, 1994).

These very different patterns – austerity followed by prosperity, and prosperity followed by recession – and the contrasting labour market conditions faced by the two different baby boom cohorts have affected their respective life chances and influenced the course of their lives. As well as influencing employment histories and the ability to secure an adequate income in later life, these experiences may also affect the two groups' expectations of employment, the welfare state and life in general. As we shall see, the trend towards greater inequality will be a persistent theme throughout the lives of the second baby boomers.

In Chapter 1, Jane Falkingham identifies the baby boom cohorts and examines why they should be of concern for social policy analysts and planners – in terms of both income support in later life and the need for social care. The remainder of the chapter is concerned with the demography of the baby boomers. Marriage and childbearing are increasingly being postponed and in many cases may be forgone altogether. The increasing propensity to divorce also means that the baby boomers are more likely to experience a spell of lone parenthood and to live alone in old age. The implications of these changes in family building, and the emergence of complex family structures, both for the ability to accumulate resources and for the baby boomers as providers and recipients of informal care, are then drawn out in subsequent chapters.

Chris Phillipson, in Chapter 2, examines the work experiences of the baby boomers to date and assesses their future employment prospects. There have been significant changes in the types of job on offer to the baby boomers, especially those from the second wave, as compared with previous cohorts. Gone is the security of 'a job for life' and smooth career progression. Instead, the younger baby boomers can expect to have more than one career and to spend more time in temporary, transitional and part-time employment. As a result, he argues, future policies about the employment and training of older workers must reflect and adapt to a more flexible labour market, particularly in the key areas of recruitment, career progression and career exit.

The implications of these labour market trends for financial resources in later life are developed further in Chapter 3 by Ruth Hancock. Higher real earnings, increased occupational and personal pension coverage, greater participation by women in the labour force and more home ownership all suggest that the baby boomers can look forward to a financially secure retirement. But she warns that such optimism may be premature. Men's working lives have been shortened at both ends by later school-leaving and earlier retirement. And most of the increase for baby boom women will be in part-time and temporary jobs, which are less likely to provide an employer's pension. Given that there will be more people in retirement relative to a smaller working population, the challenge will be to ensure a minimum standard of living in retirement whilst avoiding the least desirable aspects of targeting, such as stigma and non-take-up of benefits.

How far resources will go in later life will in part be a function of the baby boomers' need for health and social care and whether they will be expected to pay for that care. These questions are the focus of the next three chapters. Gillian Dalley, in Chapter 4, begins by looking at the future health status and health care needs of the baby boomers. The evidence regarding prospects for a healthier old age is mixed. On the one hand the baby boomers have benefited, and will continue to benefit, from changes in the environment, nutrition, safer work practices and more effective public health. But they face new risks, including BSE, *E. coli*, new 'designer' drugs such as Ecstasy and AIDS. Furthermore, the disparities in employment experience within the cohorts themselves may also have an impact on health, and be reflected in greater inequalities. This will be exacerbated if the trend towards private provision continues, with the abandonment of the principle of free health care for everyone.

This theme is continued by Jane Lewis in Chapter 5, who considers the type and extent of community care the baby boomers might expect to find. She argues that resource constraints have been the primary force behind recent policy developments, and if policy continues to evolve along current lines, more of the baby boomers may find themselves having to pay for nursing home care and domiciliary services. The alternative for those who do not meet the eligibility criteria for collectively provided formal care, and who cannot pay for it themselves, is the informal care sector, which is examined in Chapter 6.

The baby boomers are more likely than previous generations to have surviving parents (and grandparents), and a significant minority may find themselves providing care to an older relative. Chapter 6 looks at how this caring experience may affect their economic, social and physical well-being and concludes that for many women this experience will lead to lower resources later in life. As well as becoming providers of informal care, the baby boomers may subsequently be recipients of informal care. Looking at the likely influences on the demand for, and supply of, informal care in 2020, there is a clear tension between the shift towards private domiciliary care and increased charging for state support services (both of which will tend to increase demand for informal care), and demographic and labour market trends that tend to reduce the supply of informal care. It is far from clear that the informal care sector will be able to meet the demands placed on it.

In addition to health and social care, the ageing baby boomers will need a home, and in Chapter 7 Robin Means considers their likely housing future. More baby boomers will be owner-occupiers than among today's older population. But baby boomers on low income will continue to rely on social housing. Again if policy continues to develop along current lines, inequality is likely to increase. Older renters may face growing insecurity as rents rise, disrepair problems multiply and entitlement to housing benefit becomes increasingly uncertain.

The baby boomers will face a new set of opportunities and challenges, different from those of today's older people. They were born into and grew up in a different social, economic and technological environment. They were the first generations to benefit from the welfare state in terms of education and health. Their expectations of retirement and the welfare state will be different. By their sheer size the baby boomers constitute an important electoral force. Future governments will be wise to recognise the potential of this political 'muscle'.

The world the baby boomers retire into will also be different. Most notably, technology will have transformed the workplace and the home. 'Smart' houses, aids and adaptations and communication via the Internet will transform daily life. Not all the baby boomers will, however, be in a position to reap the benefits of the new technology. Changes in the labour market may result in a more polarised society, with a widening divide between those who are resourced and those who are under-resourced.

The implications of these trends, both for central government policy and for the baby boomers themselves in retirement, are drawn out in Chapter 8. Key issues to be addressed by a future policy agenda are discussed. What is clear is the need for long-term planning for the baby boomers in retirement – and, critically, planning should start now.

1 Who are the baby boomers? A demographic profile

Jane Falkingham

This book is primarily concerned with the future of the baby boomers and their prospects in retirement. However, the position of many in later life will be governed by decisions and actions taken earlier in their lifetimes. It is useful, therefore, to look first at who the baby boomers are, how many of them are likely retire and some of the characteristics of their life courses to date. In particular, this chapter focuses on the demographic behaviour of the baby boom generations.

We begin by identifying the cohorts that constitute the baby boomers, both in Britain and elsewhere. Next we examine the relative size of these baby boom cohorts compared to those groups born both before and after them, and highlight the implications for social policy of these large birth cohorts moving through the population. This sets the scene for much of the discussion in subsequent chapters concerning both financial and social support for the baby boomers later on in life.

The family remains the most important provider of social care to today's elders, and, unless there is a radical shift in the locus of care, this is still likely to be the case when the baby boomers themselves are old. Thus, the remainder of the chapter details the patterns of partnership and family formation among the baby boomers to date and discusses how changes in the propensity to marry, have children and divorce are all likely to have important consequences for future patterns of care. Finally, we touch on the implications for social policy that may arise as a result of the differences in the ethnic composition of the baby boomers as compared with today's elders.

▪ Who are the baby boomers?

Figure 1.1 shows the trend in the number of births annually in the UK over the period 1931–94. Two separate peaks are clearly distinguishable. Immediately following the end of World War 2 the birth rate shot up. In 1946 the number of births in the UK reached 955,000 and in 1947 over 1 million babies were born.

After the initial rise following the war, and unlike the experience of North America, the annual number of births in the UK then dropped back down to the levels experienced in the 1920s. However, the fall was only temporary and the number of births began to rise again in the late 1950s. At the start of the 1960s, the UK experienced a second baby boom, the average annual number of births in the years 1961–65 exceeding 944,000 and peaking at over 1 million in 1964. The subsequent decline was less rapid than from the previous high, the annual number of births remaining over 900,000 until 1971. Therefore Britain's second baby boom can be thought of as lasting throughout most of the 1960s, the peak years being 1961–65.

As well as being a large number at birth, more of these baby boomers can expect to survive to retirement age than have previous generations and, once in retirement, more will survive for longer.

Figure 1.1 Annual number of births, UK 1931–94

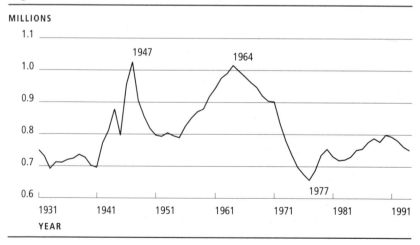

Source: OPCS Birth Statistics selected years.

16

Table 1.1 shows the improvement in expectation of life at selected ages across this century for both men and women. In 2021, when the second baby boomers will be beginning to retire, it is predicted that a man aged 60 will expect to live, on average, for a further 21.4 years and a woman for 24.9 years. This compares with 17.7 years and 21.9 years respectively for men and women aged 60 in 1991. It is also likely that these projected improvements in life expectancy may prove to be under-estimates. As Gillian Dalley discusses in Chapter 4, the baby boomers will probably be healthier in later life than are today's older people.

Table 1.1 Expectation of life at selected ages for men and women, 1901–2021

	1901	1931	1961	1991	2001	2021
Males						
At birth	45.5	57.7	67.8	73.2	75.4	77.6
1 year	54.6	62.4	69.5	73.8	75.7	77.9
10 years	60.4	65.2	69.9	73.9	75.9	78.0
20 years	61.7	66.3	70.3	74.2	76.1	78.2
40 years	66.1	69.3	71.4	75.1	77.2	79.3
60 years	73.3	74.3	74.9	77.7	79.5	81.4
80 years	84.9	84.7	85.2	86.4	87.2	88.2
Females						
At birth	49.0	61.6	73.6	78.7	80.6	82.6
1 year	56.8	65.3	75.1	79.2	80.9	82.8
10 years	62.7	67.9	75.4	79.4	81.1	83.0
20 years	64.1	69.0	75.6	79.5	81.2	83.1
40 years	68.3	71.9	76.3	80.0	81.7	83.5
60 years	74.6	76.1	78.8	81.9	83.3	84.9
80 years	85.3	85.4	86.3	88.3	89.1	90.0

Source: Government Actuary's Department.

■ Britain's baby boomers in international perspective

In other countries the baby boomers have long been a recognised social phenomenon, spawning a whole industry of sociological and economic analysis. Indeed, in the USA a report was commissioned from the Assistant Secretary of State in the Department of Health and Human Services explicitly 'regarding his responsibilities in planning for the aging of the baby boom'. However, in the UK, baby boomers as a distinct social group rarely get a mention. A recent search of the literature produced just one journal article specifically focusing on this group.

There are two reasons for this: first, unlike our 'colonial' compatriots there was not one baby boom but two, making the use of the term much more ambiguous. Secondly, these baby booms were not as pronounced as those that occurred elsewhere, making them less obvious. For example, for the first 50 years of this century Canada averaged around 250,000 births per annum, with only slight variation from year to year. However, from 1952 to 1965 between 400,000 and 500,000 children were born every year – nearly twice the previous rate. For every two children born previously there were now at least three. According to the 1966 Census, one-third of the entire population of Canada had been born in the preceding 15 years.

In contrast, whilst the number of babies born in the UK in the years 1947 and 1964 exceeded 1 million, over the entire period 1941–81 the number of births averaged about 800,000 per year. Therefore even the absolute peaks of the two baby booms constituted only an additional 25 per cent over the average for the post-war decades. In place of every four births, in these years there were five.

Figure 1.2 shows the trends in the number of births per thousand population (ie the crude birth rate) over the period 1920–80 for selected industrialised countries. Although there are some difficulties in using the crude birth rate to make comparisons between countries with different age structures, the differences in short-run trends compared with other measures, or even total annual births, is not great (Murphy, 1993).

Canada (Figure 1.2b), the USA (Figure 1.2c) and Australia (Figure 1.2d) all experienced a higher and more sustained increase in births at the end of World War 2 than in Europe. Birth rates did not fall during the 1950s as in England and Wales, but then decreased more rapidly

Figure 1.2a Births per 1,000 population; England and Wales, 1920–80

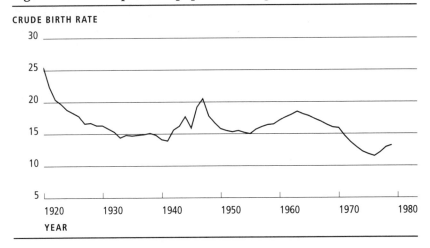

Figure 1.2b Births per 1,000 population; Canada, 1920–80

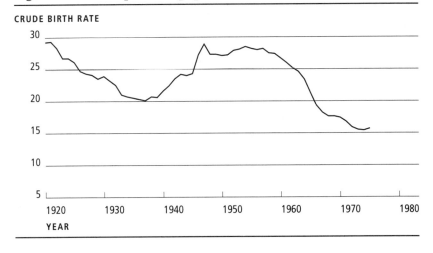

from the mid-1960s onwards. In France (Figure 1.2e) there was only a brief post-war boom, whereas in Germany there was no evidence of a baby boom at all (Figure 1.2f). Thus the experience in Britain falls somewhere between the situation in Canada, Australia and Europe.

Figure 1.2c Births per 1,000 population; USA, 1920–80

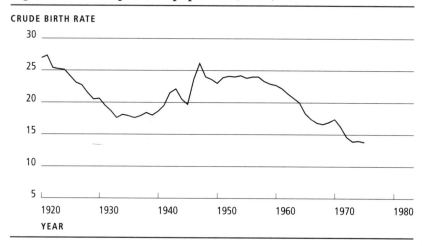

Figure 1.2d Births per 1,000 population; Australia, 1920–80

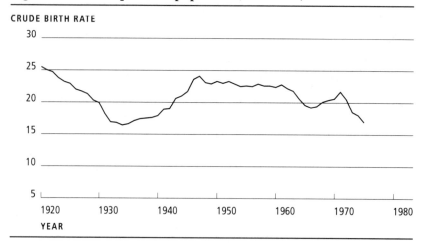

Figure 1.2e Births per 1,000 population; France, 1920–80

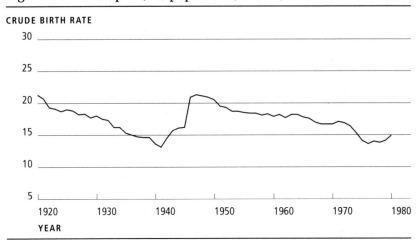

Figure 1.2f Births per 1,000 population; Germany, 1920–80

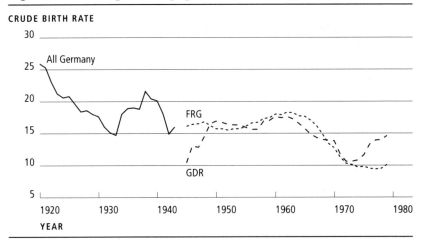

▪ The baby boomers and social policy – should we worry?

Because of their number, the baby boomers have affected, and will continue to affect, economic and social policy. The 1947 birth peak caught the country by surprise, overwhelming the infant National Health Service (NHS). When they reached school age, many had to be housed in prefabricated classrooms because there was insufficient space in the infant schools – the extra 100,000 births constituted an additional class in each and every school across the country. Similarly, schools expanded during the 1960s and early 1970s as school rolls rose, only to contract again as the birth rate fell. But whereas the first baby boom was a short sharp shock, the second involved a more gradual expansion and decline, giving planners more flexibility and time for planning.

Nowhere will such forward planning be more vital than for policy regarding the baby boomers in retirement. Table 1.2 shows the size of the baby boom generations when they reach retirement age compared with today's elders. The first baby boomers, represented by the five-year birth cohort 1946–50, will be aged 60–64 in 2010 and will constitute 1 million more people than the same age group in 1995. And when the second baby boomers reach the same age in 2025, there will be over 0.5 million more people than in 2010 and 1.6 million more than today.

Table 1.2 The size of different birth cohorts in the UK at ages 60–64 and 70–74

BIRTH COHORT	Representatives	Size at age 60–64 (millions)	Size at age 70–74 (millions)
1916–20	Iris Murdoch Dennis Healey	2.9 (1980)	2.2 (1990)
1931–35	Maggie Smith Jonathan Miller	2.8 (1995)	2.2 (2005)
1946–50	Twiggy Gordon Brown	3.8 (2010)	3.2 (2020)
1961–65	Anthea Turner Nick Leeson	4.4 (2025)	3.8 (2035)

Source: OPCS Population Trends. Projections are from 1992-based national population projections (OPCS, 1995a).

Figure 1.2e Births per 1,000 population; France, 1920–80

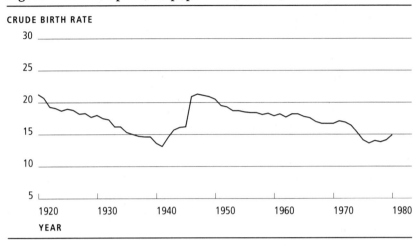

Figure 1.2f Births per 1,000 population; Germany, 1920–80

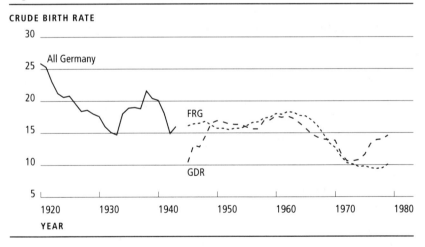

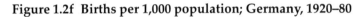

▬ The baby boomers and social policy – should we worry?

Because of their number, the baby boomers have affected, and will continue to affect, economic and social policy. The 1947 birth peak caught the country by surprise, overwhelming the infant National Health Service (NHS). When they reached school age, many had to be housed in prefabricated classrooms because there was insufficient space in the infant schools – the extra 100,000 births constituted an additional class in each and every school across the country. Similarly, schools expanded during the 1960s and early 1970s as school rolls rose, only to contract again as the birth rate fell. But whereas the first baby boom was a short sharp shock, the second involved a more gradual expansion and decline, giving planners more flexibility and time for planning.

Nowhere will such forward planning be more vital than for policy regarding the baby boomers in retirement. Table 1.2 shows the size of the baby boom generations when they reach retirement age compared with today's elders. The first baby boomers, represented by the five-year birth cohort 1946–50, will be aged 60–64 in 2010 and will constitute 1 million more people than the same age group in 1995. And when the second baby boomers reach the same age in 2025, there will be over 0.5 million more people than in 2010 and 1.6 million more than today.

Table 1.2 The size of different birth cohorts in the UK at ages 60–64 and 70–74

BIRTH COHORT	Representatives	Size at age 60–64 (millions)		Size at age 70–74 (millions)	
1916–20	Iris Murdoch Dennis Healey	2.9	(1980)	2.2	(1990)
1931–35	Maggie Smith Jonathan Miller	2.8	(1995)	2.2	(2005)
1946–50	Twiggy Gordon Brown	3.8	(2010)	3.2	(2020)
1961–65	Anthea Turner Nick Leeson	4.4	(2025)	3.8	(2035)

Source: OPCS Population Trends. Projections are from 1992-based national population projections (OPCS, 1995a).

Of equal importance for the finance of income support in later life, and for the provision of social care, is not just the relatively large size of the baby boom groups themselves – and especially the second and larger boom of the early 1960s – but also the relatively small size of the succeeding generations. The fact that the baby boom of the 1960s was followed by the baby bust of the 1970s (when fertility fell, in 1977, to an average of 1.7 children per woman) has important implications for both the availability of informal carers and for the future financing of social security in general, and of pensions in particular.

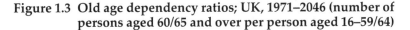

Figure 1.3 Old age dependency ratios; UK, 1971–2046 (number of persons aged 60/65 and over per person aged 16–59/64)

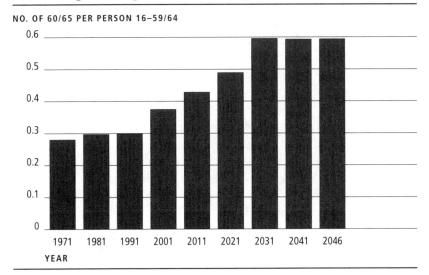

Source: OPCS Population Trends and Population Projections, 1992-based.

Figure 1.3 shows the 'Old Age Dependency Ratio' – the total number of women aged 60 and over and of men aged 65 and over divided by the number of people aged 16–59/64. The latter is taken to be representative of the working age population, whilst the former is representative of the older population whom the working age population has to support. Although this is a crude index*, it nevertheless provides a useful summary of the relative size of different age groups in

* For a critique of such measures, see Falkingham (1989).

the population. In 1991 there were just under 30 people of pensionable age per 100 people aged 16–59/64. By 2011, when the first baby boomers begin to retire, this figure will have risen to 43 per 100. But by 2031, by which time virtually all of the first and second baby boomers will have retired, there will be nearly 60 people of pensionable age per 100 people of working age – double the number in 1991! Because both the basic pension and the state earnings-related pension scheme (SERPS) are funded on a 'pay-as-you-go' basis (ie through the contributions of the current workforce rather than through the savings of previous contributions), a fall in the ratio of workers to pensioners implies either a reduction in the value of pensions or an increase in contributions (taxes) or some combination of the two (Johnson and Falkingham, 1992)*. The options facing any future government are discussed by Ruth Hancock in Chapter 3.

Financial support in later life is only one side of the coin. The changing balance between different age groups will also affect the supply of, and demand for, social care. Figure 1.4 presents what may be thought of as a 'Social Care Dependency Ratio' – the number of people aged 75 and over, taken to represent the population potentially in need of care, divided by the number of women aged 45–59, taken to represent the potential supply of informal carers. Obviously these groups are only crude approximations of the true demand and supply of informal care. Many men provide important care services. Similarly, many people aged over 75 are in excellent health, whilst some younger people may be less fortunate. However, as Maria Evandrou has shown (1992), women are more likely than men to be the main carer, and are more likely perform arduous personal care tasks. And most recipients of informal care are aged over 75.

What is immediately obvious from Figure 1.4 is that there will be a marked shift in the balance between the supply of and the demand for informal care in the next 50 years. In 1991 there were 84 people aged 75 and over per 100 women aged 45–59. This ratio will improve up to the year 2011 as the second baby boomers move into the peak ages as *providers* of informal care, whilst the first baby boom cohort will not

---

* Note that the increase in revenue can come either from increasing the contribution rate for a given number of contributors or from increasing the number of contributors (eg through higher labour force participation of women or lower unemployment).

Figure 1.4 Number of persons aged 75 and over per woman aged 45–59; UK, 1971–2046

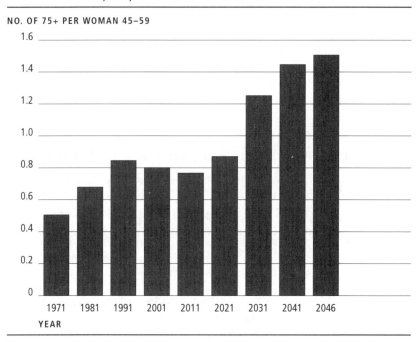

NO. OF 75+ PER WOMAN 45–59

YEAR

Source: OPCS Population Trends and Population Projections, 1992-based.

yet be in the age range where they will be in need of care. But by 2031 the position will be reversed and by 2041 both the first and second baby boom cohorts will be aged over 75. It is expected that in 2046 there will be a staggering 150 people aged 75 and over per 100 women aged 45–59. This is the result of both larger numbers of older people and smaller numbers of potential carers. These potential carers are today's children, of whom many are the children of the second baby boomers.

Thus, despite not facing such extreme changes in the age composition of the population as will be experienced when the Canadian or American baby boomers enter old age, the data presented in Figures 1.3 and 1.4 suggest that the sooner we begin to plan for the old age of the British baby boomers the better. In order to do so it is useful to look at the experiences of the baby boom generations so far, and to see how they are likely to shape that future. Other chapters examine their employment experience and the prospects for health and resources in later life. The remainder of this chapter therefore focuses on the demographic characteristics and behaviour of the baby boom cohorts to date, outlining those acquired so far and predicting future patterns. By looking at the experiences of the current older population we will also attempt to shed some light on how tomorrow's elderly may differ from today's.

■ The demography of the baby boom cohorts

In the Introduction it was stated that we should be careful about treating the experience of the two baby boom cohorts as synonymous. Nowhere is this more true than with regard to their demographic characteristics and patterns of partnership and family formation.

Marriage and partnership

Kiernan and Eldridge (1985), in their analysis of marriage patterns, found that the people born in the immediate post-war period (1946–50) are the most married this century. However, for those born after 1955, including the second baby boom, there has been a sustained decline in first marriage rates at every age (Haskey, 1993a). Figure 1.5 presents the proportion of women and men who had never married by certain ages for four single-year birth cohorts, using data from the Office of Population Censuses and Surveys (OPCS) Marriage Statistics (OPCS, 1995b). The first baby boom can be thought of as being represented by those born in 1947, the peak birth year. Those born in 1958 characterise the start of the second baby boom, whilst those born in 1964 represent the peak of the second boom.

There has been a clear shift in the timing of marriage, marriage occurring on average at earlier ages among the 1947 cohort than among those born in 1931. However, for later generations the age at marriage has shifted upwards again. Women and men from the second baby boom have tended to stay single for longer (ie marry at later ages) than those born in 1931 and 1947.

Figure 1.5 Proportion of (a) women and (b) men who remain unmarried, by birth cohort (England and Wales)

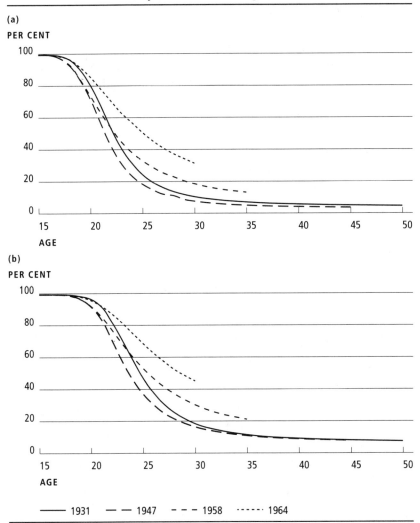

Source: OPCS Marriage Statistics Series FM2.

27

Of course, the fact that fewer of the second baby boomers have married does not necessarily mean that they are without partners. Part of the recent trend towards later marriage reflects an increase in the proportion of couples who live together before their marriage. John Haskey (1995) shows that seven out of ten first marriages in the early 1990s were preceded by premarital cohabitation, compared with only one in ten in the early 1970s. In addition, there has been a rise in the duration of cohabitation, indicating that some couples may prefer long-term cohabitation as an alternative to legal marriage. In 1994, 30 per cent of unmarried men and 25 per cent of unmarried women aged 30–34 were in cohabiting unions (OPCS, 1996).

Nevertheless, despite higher rates of cohabitation there also appears to be a growing tendency for those in the second baby boom to live outside *any* form partnership (Haskey, 1995). Kiernan and Wicks (1990) have estimated that the trend towards more cohabiting accounts for only one-third of the decline in the proportion of women ever married at ages 25–29 in the 1980s (ie among the second baby boomers). The balance remained outside of a union. A key question is what proportion of the second baby boomers will never have married or formed a union by the time they enter old age?

OPCS produce (unpublished) projections of marital status (including people in a long-term cohabiting union), and these are included in Figure 1.6. There *is* expected to be an element of catching up, with a significant fall in the proportion of never married or seriously cohabiting between the ages of 30 and 40 among the 1964 cohort. But at age 50, 12 per cent of women and 18 per cent of men in the second baby boom group are predicted to still not have formed a permanent union, compared with only 5 per cent of women and 9 per cent of men in the 1947 group. Given that the most important source of practical and emotional support for the current older population is from their spouse or partner (OPCS, 1996), this trend towards living outside a union may have important ramifications for future patterns of care.

Figure 1.6 Proportion of (a) women and (b) men who remained unmarried by ages 30, 40 and 50 (England and Wales)

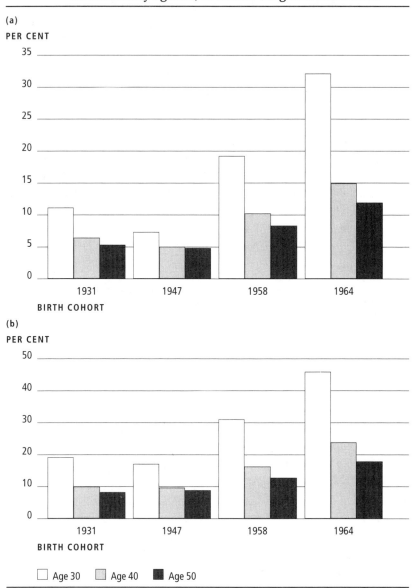

Source: OPCS Marriage Statistics Series FM2 and unpublished 1992-based marital status projections.

Patterns of family formation

As Maria Evandrou discusses in Chapter 6, the other main source of social support in later life are children. The two baby boom groups have also experienced very different patterns of childbearing. Just as there was a move towards earlier marriage in the 1947 group and later marriage in the 1964 group, so there has been a change in the timing of the first birth: *earlier* childbearing among the first baby boomers and then back towards *later* childbearing among the second.

Figure 1.7 shows the proportion of women (born in 1931, 1947, 1958 and 1964) who have never had a child by a particular age. By age 25 only 37 per cent of the women born in 1947 had not given birth, whereas 60 per cent of the women born in 1964 remained childless at the same age. There has been a similar experience elsewhere in Europe. David Coleman (1995) shows that, in the Netherlands, 18 per cent of women were still childless by their mid-30s in 1992, and the proportions rise to 20 per cent in Austria and 21 per cent in Switzerland.

Figure 1.7 Proportion of women remaining childless by birth cohort

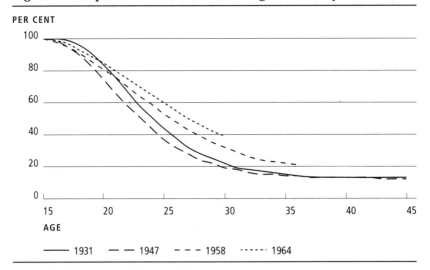

Source: OPCS Marriage Statistics Series FM1.

Some of this shift to later, and less, childbearing can be related to the fall in marriage – traditionally taken to be a prerequisite to having a family. However, births *outside* of marriage have increased sharply over the last two decades from just under 10 per cent of all births in 1977 to 32 per cent in 1993 (Babb and Bethune, 1995). This reflects the changes that have occurred in marriage patterns and the increase in cohabiting unions. In recent years, four out of five births outside marriage have been registered by both parents, of whom most were living at the same address.

The key question is: what is the likely future pattern of childbearing for the second baby boomers? Women born in 1920 experienced the highest levels of childlessness of any cohort this century, with 21 per cent still childless at the age of 45. Looking at the trend to date for women in the 1964 cohort, it seems likely that they will exceed this level of childlessness. But the second baby boom women are still in their reproductive years. Recent data indicate that the number of births is rising among women in their 30s (Jones, 1992), so it may be that the second baby boom women are *postponing* having children rather than not having them at all. However, for the group as a whole, it is unlikely that later childbearing will fully compensate for the shortfall in births at younger ages. Levels of fertility fall with age, and, as the average age at first birth rises, so more women who were previously fertile may find themselves unable to conceive when they want to start a family (Coleman, 1996).

Figure 1.8 predicts that, by the end of their reproductive span, 21 per cent of second baby boom women will remain childless. Although this figure is high compared with only 13 per cent of first baby boom women, the graph shows that such levels of childlessness are not unprecedented. However, *more* of the people born in 1964 will survive to old age than have those of the early 1920s, and more will live longer in old age. In the past, childless older people have been more likely to enter institutional care than have people with children (Grundy and Harrop, 1991; Allen et al, 1992). It remains to be seen what will happen to the childless baby boomers.

There has also been a fall in average family size. Although a large proportion of women born in the early 1920s remained childless, nearly 40 per cent of the women born in 1920 who had children, had

Figure 1.8 Actual or predicted distribution of number of children per woman by year of birth, 1920–80

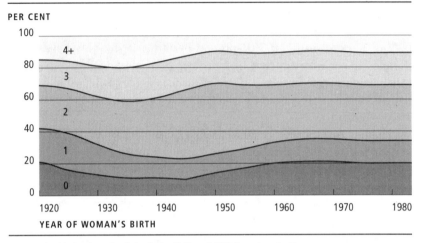

Source: OPCS Marriage Statistics Series FM1 and 1992-based projections.

three or more (see Figure 1.8). The average number of liveborn children per woman was 2. For women born in 1945, the corresponding figure is 2.2, but for women born in 1965 it is anticipated that they will have, on average, only 1.9 children. However, other changes in the family, and in particular the increasing tendency towards divorce and remarriage, may mean that more of the second baby boomers have step-children as well as natural children. Below we look at trends in family break-up and reconstitution among the baby boomers.

Divorce

The rise in divorce constitutes one of the most dramatic changes in family life in Britain this century. In 1993 there were 180,000 divorces, nearly *seven times* the number in 1961 (CSO, 1996). The increase in divorce has accompanied a number of major changes in the law – the most notable being the 1969 Divorce Reform Act, which came into effect on 1 January 1971 in England and Wales. This Act introduced a solitary ground for divorce of the 'irretrievable breakdown of marriage', established by proving one or more of five 'facts': unreasonable behaviour, adultery, desertion, having been separated for two years if both parties agree and separated for five years if there is not mutual consent. The Act marked a watershed in the way society viewed divorce – from 1971 it was no longer necessary to have a 'guilty partner'. The Matrimonial and Family Proceedings Act 1984 further reduced the minimum period after marriage that a petition for divorce could be filed.

The effect of the 1969 Act is clearly visible in Figure 1.9. People born in 1931 were aged 40 when the Act came into effect, and the proportion ever divorced among this cohort increased more sharply between the ages of 40 and 50. Younger generations have experienced progressively greater rates of marital breakdown. Data for the 1964 cohort go only up to the age of 30 but, at first sight, it seems that the trend towards divorce may be in retreat. However, we have seen that a smaller proportion of this group have actually married and therefore fewer are actually at risk of experiencing a divorce. Among those of the 1964 cohort who *had* married, 18 per cent of women and 15 per cent of men had already seen that marriage break up by their thirtieth birthday*. The higher divorce rate among the baby boomers and the fact that they are divorcing at younger ages have a number of important implications for the types of family life experienced by this cohort.

Lone parenthood

Divorces involving children under 16, and especially children under 5, have become more common in recent years. This, coupled with the smaller proportions marrying and higher rates of childbirth outside marriage, means that people in the younger cohorts are much more likely than those in the older cohorts to have experienced an episode of lone parenthood. Evandrou and Falkingham (1997), using data from the General Household Survey (GHS) over the period 1974–93, found that the incidence of lone motherhood at a given age increased

---

* The proportion of women who had divorced by each age is generally slightly higher than the corresponding proportion of men. This is the effect of wives generally being younger than their husbands. For a more detailed account of cohort divorce rates, see Haskey (1993a).

Figure 1.9 Proportion of (a) women and (b) men who ever divorced, by birth cohort (England and Wales)

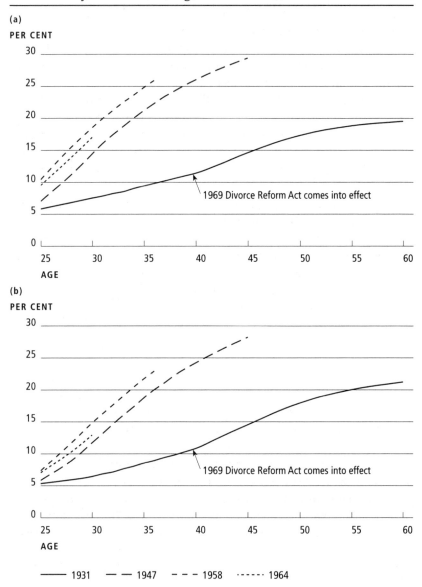

(a)

PER CENT

1969 Divorce Reform Act comes into effect

AGE

(b)

PER CENT

1969 Divorce Reform Act comes into effect

AGE

—— 1931   — — 1947   – – – 1958   ····· 1964

dramatically between women born in 1946–50 and 1961–65: 12 per cent of women from the 1961–65 cohort were lone mothers at age 30, compared with just 5 per cent of the 1946–50 cohort at the same age. Lone parenthood is, of course, not confined to women, although lone-mother families are ten times as numerous as lone-father families. However, John Haskey (1994a) shows that the number of lone fathers has more than doubled in the last twenty years. Most of this increase has occurred among men from the baby boom generations, the median age of lone fathers being 43 in 1990 (Haskey, 1993b).

Although the second baby boomers will cease to be lone parents – either through remarriage or from their children reaching 16 – long before they reach old age, the fact that a greater proportion of them will have experienced an episode of lone parenthood is likely to have some impact during retirement. Lone motherhood is associated with lower living standards both at the time (Haskey, 1994a; Millar, 1994) *and* across the life course. Evandrou and Falkingham (1995) identified experience of an episode of lone parenthood as an important predictor of low lifetime income. In particular, interrupted employment histories and lower wages when in work will be reflected in lower pension rights in later life. Such links are explored by Ruth Hancock in Chapter 3.

Remarriage and 'reconstituted families'

More and younger divorce also mean that more of the baby boomers are 'at risk' of remarriage and thus time spent in a *reconstituted family*. In the early decades of this century, remarriage was usually after being widowed – which most often. but not invariably, occurred at older ages. In contrast, in more recent years most people who remarry have done so after divorce (around 90 per cent in 1990), and most of these partners are in their 30s or early 40s (Haskey, 1993a). Younger remarriage makes the presence of children, and thus step-children, more likely. In addition, there is evidence that more divorced couples are choosing to cohabit rather than remarry – resulting in even more step-families. It is estimated that in 1990–92 20 per cent of all cohabiting couple families were step-families, and that these accounted for about one-third of all step-families (Haskey, 1994b).

Historical data on the proportion of children who are step-children are rare. It is interesting, though, that two of the key data sets provide some evidence about the experience of the baby boomers *themselves* as step-children. Data from the National Study of Health and Development, which followed a group of people born in the same week in 1946, show that 3.5 per cent of them were step-children at the age of 15 (Douglas, 1970). Similar information from the 1958 National Child Development Study shows that 4–5 per cent of all those born during a given week in 1958 were living as step-children at the age of 16 (Ferri, 1984; Kiernan, 1992). Linda Clarke (1992), using data from the General Household Survey (GHS), has estimated that, by 1984/5, 9 per cent of all children under 16 of women aged 18–49 (ie of both baby boom cohorts) were step-children.

All these figures are cross-sectional, referring to one point in time. Of course, children living with one or both of their natural parents today may become a step-child at some future point. John Haskey (1994b) has calculated the proportion of today's children (ie the children of the second baby boomers) who could expect to be a step-child at some stage before reaching their sixteenth birthday He estimates that around 6 per cent of all children will have become step-children of a married couple and 7 per cent of a cohabiting couple. Strictly speaking, these percentages should not be added together, because some children may experience both states. Nevertheless, it provides an interesting pointer to the number of baby boomers who may have extended families. As Maria Evandrou discusses in Chapter 6, the increase in the number of step-children raises interesting questions about the future nature of family ties and obligations, and in particular the availability and willingness of step-children to care for their older step-parent.

Living alone in later life

Finally, the increased tendency to divorce may have important implications for the living arrangements of the baby boomers in later life. Table 1.3 presents unpublished data from the OPCS 1992-based forecasts of marital status. The OPCS forecasts of marital status reach only the year 2022, and so do not allow us to look at the likely plight of the second baby boomers beyond the age of 60. Nevertheless, some interesting trends emerge. A greater proportion of the baby boomers will be divorced or separated by the time they are 60 than were those aged 60 in 1991, and fewer will be widowed. But the fall in widowhood will not be sufficient to offset the rise in the proportion divorced, with the net effect of an increase in the proportion not living in a union at the age of 60 of between 10 per cent (for women) and 15 per cent (for men) for those born 1961 as compared to 1931.

Table 1.3 Marital status at age 60 and 75 for selected birth cohorts

YEAR OF BIRTH	Single		Married		Divorced/Separated		Widowed	
	W	M	W	M	W	M	W	M
At age 60								
1931	6	8	71	82	8	6	15	4
1947	4	8	68	76	15	13	13	3
1961	10	14	61	67	20	16	10	3
At age 75								
1931	5	7	39	73	8	6	47	15
1947	4	7	35	68	16	13	45	12

W, women; M, men

Source: OPCS population projections by marital status, 1992-based (unpublished).

Given the shift to later and fewer marriages and increasing divorce, what proportion of the British baby boomers are likely to live alone in later life? Following the methodology used by Hancock et al (1995), by applying the current proportions of people in different living arrangements within each marital status from the 1993 GHS, to the 1992-based projections of marital status, we can estimate the proportion of each cohort that will be living alone at the ages of 60 and 75. The results are shown in Figure 1.10. Over two in every five people born between 1946 and 1950 will be living alone by the age of 75. Moreover, it is predicted that a quarter of second baby boomers (1961–65) will already be lone householders by the time they are 60. Given that experience so far indicates that the main increase in living alone occurs between the ages of 60 and 75, it is likely that, by the age of 75, an even greater proportion of the second baby boom will be living alone. This has important implications for the provision of social

Figure 1.10 Proportion living alone at age 60 and 75, by birth cohort

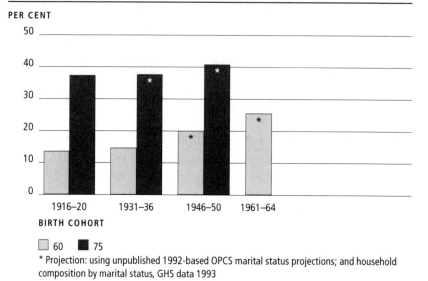

PER CENT

BIRTH COHORT

☐ 60 ■ 75

* Projection: using unpublished 1992-based OPCS marital status projections; and household composition by marital status, GHS data 1993

services. In 1994 people over 75 years of age and living alone were twice as likely to have a local authority home help and four times as likely to receive meals-on-wheels compared to those who were living with their spouse (OPCS, 1996). The implications for both the demand for and the supply of social care are discussed further in Chapter 6.

Ethnicity and the baby boomers

The final key demographic characteristic whereby the baby boomers in retirement may be expected to differ from today's older population concerns their ethnic mix. Table 1.4 presents data on the ethnic composition of different birth cohorts drawn from the 1991 Census. Among today's 'middle aged' older people (those born 1916–20) only about 1 per cent classify themselves as being of minority ethnic origin. However, the proportion of 'non-white' increases with each successive cohort, reflecting both the pattern of migration into Britain and the family-building patterns of different groups. Of the second baby boom generation, around 3 per cent are of Black origin, 2.5 per cent south

Asian and 1.5 per cent from 'Other' groups. This changing ethnic mix may have implications for the types of health and social care required in later life.

Table 1.4 Ethnic composition of selected birth cohorts, 1991

BIRTH COHORT	White		Black[a]		South Asian[b]		Other groups[c]	
	M	W	M	W	M	W	M	W
1916–20	98.6	99.0	0.5	0.3	0.7	0.4	0.3	0.2
1931–35	95.6	96.6	1.6	1.3	2.2	1.6	0.7	0.6
1946–50	96.0	95.5	0.8	1.0	2.1	2.2	1.1	1.3
1961–65	93.3	92.7	2.6	3.0	2.5	2.8	1.6	1.6

a Black includes Black Caribbean, Black African and Black 'other'.
b South Asian includes Indian, Pakistani and Bangladeshi.
c Other groups includes Chinese, Asian and 'other'.

W, women; M, men

Source: 1991 Census; note that age–sex–ethnic groups were weighted by published weighting factors to 'correct' for estimated under-coverage of each group in the 1991 Census.

▪ Summary

- More of the baby boomers can expect to survive to retirement age than have previous generations and, once in retirement, more will survive for longer.

- In 2010 there will be 1 million more people aged 60–64 than in 1995. And when the second baby boomers reach the same age in 2025 there will be half a million more again.

- The large size of the baby boom cohorts, combined with smaller 'baby bust' cohorts of the 1970s and 1980s, means that there will be increased pressure on both the financing of pay-as-you-go pensions and the provision of social care:
  - by 2031 there will be nearly 60 people of pensionable age for every 100 people of working age – double the number in 1991;
  - by 2041 there will be 145 people aged 75 and over for every 100 women aged 45–59.

- Greater proportions of the second baby boomers will never have married or formed a long-term cohabiting union by the time they reach age 50 than have previous generations.

- Fewer will have had children, and those who do have children will have fewer children of their own.

- With increased divorce and remarriage, more baby boomers will have experienced periods of lone parenthood and of step-parenthood.

- More baby boomers will live outside a union in old age than in previous generations, and more will live alone.

- A greater proportion of the second baby boomers are from minority ethnic groups than ever before.

2 Employment and training: planning for 2020 and beyond

Chris Phillipson

Employment and training for older workers have emerged as key issues in social and economic policy. The reasons for this are at least threefold. First, as the baby boomers age, older people represent an increasingly important segment of the population. It is estimated that, by the year 2020, 40 per cent of the total population in Great Britain will be aged 50 and over (38 per cent of men and 42 per cent of women), compared with 31 per cent of the total population in this age group in 1971 (28 per cent of men and 34 per cent of women). Second, within this ageing population, older workers will become an increasingly significant group – over one in four workers will be aged 50-plus by the year 2020, compared with one in five in 1990. Third, concern over the financing of retirement is now a major issue both for individuals and for governments. Individuals face the pressure of reduced years in work and increased years in retirement, which produces diminished opportunities for acquiring savings and pension rights. Governments face the prospect of a larger post-retirement population, but with reduced tax revenues to provide appropriate levels of financial support.

These developments raise important questions about the future employment prospects of the baby boom cohorts. The creation of new employment opportunities, and the protection of existing jobs, is likely to be an important strategy for tackling some of the pressures associated with demographic change. However, much will have to be done to translate this objective into a feasible set of programmes. The focus of this chapter is on the challenge, for government and employers, arising from an ageing workforce. This is a positive development, which means more people with a variety of skills and talents. Harnessing these will, however, require commitment and imagination in policies and programmes.

The aim of this chapter is to provide a framework for the debate, examining the range of ideas that will need to be developed to help older workers in the twenty-first century. The chapter begins with an assessment of the labour market position of the baby boomers today; there follows a review of some key developments likely to take place over the next two decades; finally, there is an outline of policies for the future, especially regarding initiatives in the key areas of recruitment, career progression and career exit.

■ Older workers in the labour market

Older workers in Britain experienced a variety of pressures in the 1980s and through into the 1990s. In the early and middle parts of the 1980s they were being urged to leave the workforce as soon as possible, as a way of coping with high unemployment and large numbers of school-leavers (Laczko and Phillipson, 1991). By the early 1990s, however, concern about the ageing of the workforce shifted the debate towards how to stem the flow of older workers out of employment, and to remove age barriers in areas such as recruiting and retaining staff (Trinder, Hulme and McCarthy 1992; Taylor and Walker, 1993).

Over the past two decades there have been significant changes in the shape of the labour force (Blackwell, 1992; Bone et al, 1992). First, there has been the fall in the number of young people entering the workforce: in 1993 there were about 1 million fewer 16- to 19-year-olds in the population than there were in 1983, a fall of 28 per cent. Second, there has been the accelerating exit of older people from paid employment (Table 2.1). In 1971, 93 per cent of men aged 55–59 were in the labour force (ie *economically active*: either in employment or unemployed and looking for work). By spring 1994 this figure had declined to 76 per cent. In 1994 around 51 per cent of men aged 60–64 were economically active compared with 83 per cent in 1971.

In contrast to the experience of older men, older women have generally become more active in the labour market over the past three decades. In 1971, 51 per cent of women aged 55–59 were working (outside the home). By spring 1994 this figure had risen to 56 per cent. For women aged 60–64, the figures from 1981 to 1995 also suggest a slight increase. As with men, however, economic activity among women aged 65 and over declined from 6.3 per cent in 1971 to 3.4 per cent in 1994.

Table 2.1 **Economic activity rates for older women and men in Britain, 1971–95**

AGE	Estimates					Projection
	1971	1975	1981	1985	1991	1995
Women						
25–34	45.5	51.8	56.4	62.4	69.9	71.9
35–44	59.7	66.1	68.0	72.0	76.8	77.1
45–54	62.0	66.3	68.0	69.6	72.8	76.0
55–59	50.9	52.4	53.4	52.2	54.5	56.1
60–64	28.8	28.6	23.3	18.9	24.1	25.6
65+	6.3	4.9	3.7	3.0	3.1	3.1
Men						
25–34	94.6	94.9	95.4	96.2	95.9	94.6
35–44	96.2	96.4	96.0	96.7	95.7	93.2
45–54	95.7	96.1	94.8	93.0	91.6	90.5
55–59	93.0	93.0	89.4	82.2	80.8	76.4
60–64	82.9	82.4	69.3	55.4	54.1	50.7
65–69	30.4	25.9	16.3	14.5	15.2	14.9
70+	10.9	8.3	6.5	5.3	4.8	3.8

Source: Employment Department, *Employment Gazette* (April) 1995.

■ Employment and the baby boom cohorts

These general trends may be illustrated further by dividing all the age groups into five-year bands and distinguishing between those employed and those registered as unemployed (using ILO/OECD definitions). The figures for men are given in Table 2.2, taking the period 1984–94 and selected years in between. The sharp downturn in the employment of older workers is clear, with just 45 per cent of men aged 60–64 actually in employment in 1994.

The figures also confirm, albeit with the limitations of cross-sectional data, the importance of the 50-plus age barrier, with 86 per cent of the first baby boomers (aged 45–49 in 1994) in employment, compared with just 78 per cent of those aged 50–54. Clearly, as the group now in their mid- to late 40s passes through to their 50s over the next few years, age discrimination in employment is likely to become a significant issue in their lives (Itzin and Phillipson, 1993).

Table 2.2 Estimated economic activity rates of men in Great Britain (per cent) (ILO/OECD definitions)

AGE (years)	1984		1988		1991		1994	
	In employ-ment	Unem-ployed	In employ-ment	Unem-ployed	In employ-ment	Unem-ployed	In employ-ment	Unem-ployed
20–24	73	17	79	11	75	13	69	15
25–29	84	12	87	9	86	9	83	11
30–34	86	10	90	7	88	8	85	10
35–39	89	8	90	6	89	7	86	9
40–44	88	8	90	6	90	6	86	7
45–49	87	8	88	6	89	5	86	7
50–54	85	7	83	7	82	7	78	9
55–59	74	9	73	8	74	7	67	9
60–64	51	6	49	6	49	5	45	6
65–69	13	1	11	1	14	1	13	1
70+	5	0	5	0	5	0	4	0

Source: British Labour Force Survey.

The second group of baby boomers are also likely to encounter problems. Those born at the height of the boom entered the labour market in the early to mid-1980s and have clearly been directly affected by the recession in this period. Among men aged 25–29 in 1994, 11 per cent are unemployed, with a further 6 per cent defined as economically inactive; the figures for those aged 30–34 are 10 per cent and 5 per cent. These second baby boomers face a dual problem in terms of their experience of work. First, being a member of a large generation (in a context of high unemployment) is likely to reduce the level of lifetime earnings. Second, this group is experiencing the full extent of industrial change, with the growth of flexible labour markets, the decline of the manufacturing industry and the expansion in part-time working (Burrows and Loader, 1994).

The impact of part-time working is clearly illustrated in the figures for women (Table 2.3). The growth in this type of employment was especially strong among women in the 1950s and 1960s birth cohorts and is likely to be reinforced as these people re-enter the labour

Table 2.3 Estimated economic activity rates of women in Great Britain (per cent) (ILO/OECD definitions)

AGE (years)	1984			1988			1991		
	Full time	Part- time	Unem- ployed	Full time	Part- time	Unem- ployed	Full time	Part- time	Unem- ployed
20–24	52	8	11	54	10	8	55	10	7
25–29	36	17	9	40	19	8	44	19	6
30–34	25	27	7	29	32	7	33	35	5
35–39	26	36	6	29	38	6	33	36	5
40–44	31	36	6	35	38	4	37	37	4
45–49	32	36	5	34	38	3	38	35	3
50–54	29	33	4	30	33	4	33	32	3
55–59	23	24	4	24	25	3	23	28	3
60–64	6	14	2	6	13	1	7	16	1
65–69	2	5	1	1	4	0	1	6	0
70+	0	1	0	0	1	0	0	1	0

Source: British Labour Force Survey.

market in their late 30s and 40s. In addition to the expansion of part-time work, there has also been an increase in the proportion of women with 'multiple employment statuses per year', which includes women who move between employment status (eg from part- to full-time, or from self-employment to employment or between employment and unemployment). This feature was commented on in one of the early reports from the British Household Panel Survey (BHPS) (Buck et al, 1994). The evidence from this survey suggests that, particularly in the most recent cohorts, growth in women's employment has been concentrated in 'irregular' jobs providing 'discontinuous' employment. This reflects, first, labour supply factors such as the problems facing employed women with small children. Second, however, it is also product of labour demand, an increasing number of employers seeking this sort of irregular employment pattern. Buck et al (1994) conclude that:

> This is what we would expect of the 'new flexible firm', which responds actively to market opportunities and avoids excess labour overhead costs either by employing casual labour (which might alternatively show up as self-employment) or by employing labour casually, laying-off, making redundant, and taking up employment again as new markets open.

The implications of this development for employment and training are taken up in more detail later in this chapter.

■ Older workers and retirement

The trends mentioned above are reflected in the changes to retirement. There are good reasons for distinguishing between early exit from employment and retirement itself (Kohli et al, 1991). *Early exit* refers to the fact that older people may have a variety of experiences and expectations after leaving what may have been their main career. For some, retirement may indeed beckon, in that they decide to leave paid employment and have no expectation of returning. Others, however, will want to have some form of work, perhaps combining part-time employment with semi-retirement. Another group may find themselves in an intermediate phase – neither employed nor properly retired; this group may not be able to afford to settle into retirement but they are likely to have difficulty finding secure and well-paid employment. Yet others will leave work after an illness or disability and will enter a period of long-term sickness before their eventual retirement at state pension age.

The diversity among older workers must be kept in mind in the following review, which focuses on the broad range of employment and training initiatives for this group.

▪ Retirement in 2020 and beyond

What developments are we likely to see emerging from the picture sketched in the preceding sections? What implications do they have for the type of work and retirement patterns that will unfold over the next 20–30 years? Answers to these questions can be provided in at least three ways: first, in terms of the likely pattern of employment activity; second, in terms of the values, attitudes and lifestyles of people retiring in the future; and third, in respect of the relationship between work and retirement.

In the area of economic activity, the then Department of Employment (Ellison, 1994) provided estimates up to 2006 (Table 2.4) based on the 1993 Labour Force Survey and 1992-based population projections. These suggest that, although the steep declines in earlier retirement are unlikely to be repeated, the majority of men aged 60–64 (ie the first baby boomers) will remain outside paid employment. By contrast, women's economic activity is likely to continue to increase, especially among those 25–44 (ie the second baby boomers and their 'successors'). For women aged 45–54 and 55–59, the upward trend continues though with much smaller rates of increase.

Lange and Atkinson (1995) suggest, on the basis of these figures, that by the early part of the next century:

- The number of post-retirement individuals will be much greater.

- The likelihood that they will have been in work in their middle age will rise too, but not dramatically.

- The number of young people who will be contributing to their retirement incomes through taxes and social transfer payments

Table 2.4 Economic activity rates for older women and men in Britain, 1996–2006

AGE	Projections			Change
	1996	2001	2006	1996–2006
Women				
45–54	75.9	77.2	78.1	+2.2
55–59	55.3	56.0	56.7	+1.4
60–64	25.6	25.8	27.0	+1.4
65+	3.5	3.4	3.4	−0.1
Men				
45–54	89.9	89.5	89.1	−0.8
55–59	74.0	74.0	74.0	0.0
60–64	50.9	46.9	45.5	−5.4
65–69	13.1	12.6	12.2	−0.9
70+	4.3	4.1	4.0	−0.3

Source: Employment Department, *Employment Gazette* (April) 1994.

(pensions, social security) will remain small, and from 2007 onwards the number of people aged 24 and younger is likely to fall even further (from 6.8 million in 2007 to 6.1 million in 2030).

- Working lifetimes will have shrunk, owing to the combined effects of extended education, falling average weekly hours and, perhaps, continuing early retirement. Thus the opportunities to accrue savings and pensions rights will contract.

For baby boomers (and especially those in the first group) reaching their later working years, the evidence suggests some form of work activity at least until their mid- to late 50s. Indeed, in demographic terms, the 50-plus group will be a highly significant group comprising nearly 26 per cent of the workforce. In general, however, the idea of permanent retirement seems relatively fixed, although government policy options in setting more flexible retirement ages may lead to greater choice in terms of patterns of exit from the labour force (see below).

A second issue concerns the divergences in employment and retirement experiences both within and between the two baby boom cohorts. Many of the first baby boomers are likely to have positive attitudes about the prospect of leaving work. Finances are, of course, crucial because they influence retirees' views about the most desirable age at which to leave paid employment (Trinder, Hulme and McCarthy, 1992). Research in the 1980s showed the importance of financial factors in shaping the retirement decision. The 1988 Office of Population, Censuses and Surveys (OPCS) retirement survey, a sample survey of people aged 55–69, asked those who had taken or expected to take late retirement their main reasons for doing so. Fifty-one per cent of men gave as their main reason 'to improve financial position'. This was the second most important reason for women; one-third of them gave this response. The most important reason for women – at 44 per cent – was 'enjoy job/working'. This was the second most important reason for men, at 22 per cent (Bone et al, 1992).

Greater security in retirement finances, however, is likely to increase the momentum to leave work as early as possible. The British Social Attitudes (BSA) survey series has provided a substantial amount of data on employment attitudes. People in employment in 1989 were asked 'If, without having to work, you had what you regarded as a reasonable living income, do you think you would still prefer to have a paid job or wouldn't you bother?' Those aged 55–64 were much less likely than any other age group to prefer a job – 64 per cent of workers aged 55 or over, compared with 72–81 per cent in other age groups. The next least committed groups were those aged 45–54 years (Witherspoon and Taylor, 1990). For the first baby boom generation the tendency to withdraw from work may well increase, for at least two reasons: first is the experience of age discrimination and job insecurity; second is the changing attitudes to retirement, with greater acceptance that this can be a positive and valued stage of life (Phillipson, 1993).

Set against this will be differences within cohorts of older workers that reflect inequalities in retirement provision and expectations regarding income in old age. The possibility of 'two nations in early retirement' has been noted by Atkinson and Sutherland (1993), where they reviewed the incomes of men in the UK aged 55–64 in 1985 compared with the same age group in 1975. The evidence suggested increasing diversity in income levels of those in the long-term sick/retired category, with the unequal coverage of occupational pensions a crucial factor driving inequalities among early retirees (for a more detailed discussion of this point, see Chapter 3). This pattern of inequality is likely to be reproduced among the first baby boomers, who, despite the advantage of an 'easier' entry into the labour market, may well experience the pressures associated with early exit along pathways that are insecure in financial terms (Kohli et al, 1991; Laczko and Phillipson, 1991). Divisions will be even more marked among the second baby boomers, reflecting the long-term impact of changes to state and occupational pensions as well the effect of extended periods of joblessness.

A third major issue concerns the changing relationship between work and retirement. A key factor here is that the 1946–50 cohort – in contrast to its predecessors – is much more likely to have some experience of flexible working hours. At present, some 9.7 million people (38 per cent of all UK workers) are part of what has been described as the 'flexible workforce' (Watson, 1994). Although workers 55 and over are currently the least likely to have 'flexible working hours' (Witherspoon and Taylor, 1990), this will almost certainly change as we move into the next century. Indeed, the likelihood is that virtually all the baby boomers will have had some experience of flexible work patterns – it may even be the dominant experience in their pre-retirement years.

In addition, developments such as those mentioned above will signal a change from the usual transition from full-time work to full-time leisure, more older workers wishing to remain in the labour force after they leave their main career job. For many this may mean part-time employment, nearly always in a new job and in some cases in a different line of work. For the first baby boomers, transitional jobs after the end of a full-time career may become an important area of recruitment for employers attempting to fill labour or skill shortages. Increasingly, employers may offer 'bridges to retirement' – jobs that follow career employment and precede permanent retirement – in their overall employment policies (Doeringer, 1990). This will require a range of new approaches to recruitment and staff development policies, some of which are analysed below.

For the second baby boomers, of course, transition jobs may become a permanent feature of work experiences. Whilst the first baby boomers are still moving through the life course on the basis of some notion of work as a lifelong career, a very different view is emerging among those in their 20s and 30s. Here, not only is lifetime employment increasingly difficult to secure, but the notion of employment in a particular type of occupation for a large part of one's life has also been transformed. For women, long-term jobs have, of course, rarely been a possibility; increasingly, however, men are beginning to experience similar fragmentation in their working lives. The remainder of this chapter examines the implications of this development in terms of an employment and training strategy.

■ An employment and training strategy for the baby boomers

Despite the growth in popularity of retirement (especially but not exclusively) among the middle classes, a strong case is likely to be heard for encouraging employment among those in their 50s and 60s. Signs of this have already been apparent in the 1990s and reflect a number of factors. First, the long-standing interest in the USA in issues relating to older workers has given rise to the idea of 'productive ageing', a theme that provides scope for devising new approaches to supporting mature and older people in the workplace (O'Reilly and Caro, 1994). Second, concern over the possibility of labour and skill shortages (underpinned by demographic change) have led governments and other agencies to mount or support campaigns around the theme of 'investing in older people at work' (Employment Department Group, 1994; Health Education Authority, 1994). Third, issues about older workers have also surfaced in campaigns regarding equal opportunities and discriminatory practices, with the public sector (local government especially) prominent in this activity (Itzin and Phillipson, 1993; Metropolitan Authorities Recruitment Agency, 1994).

Over the next ten to twenty years concern about the position of older workers is likely to intensify, as the institution of retirement is further fragmented with greater flexibility in work and retirement practices (Laczko and Phillipson, 1991; Watson, 1994). Employers and government are beginning to recognise the costs involved in failing to use mature and older workers, and are constructing a 'business' case for recruiting and retaining this group (Institute of Personnel Management, 1993).

In practical terms, research indicates that a number of different measures are being adopted to encourage the retention of workers in the cross-over stage between work (second age) and retirement (third age). Moore, Tilson and Whitting (1994) have reviewed initiatives in 22 countries in terms of:

- Efforts to encourage employers to change employment practices to make it easier to maintain the employment of older workers.

- Measures to provide older people with the skills and expertise to compete more effectively in the labour market.

- The possibility of delayed retirement options, or continued working with an employer or in a voluntary capacity in the community.

- Recruitment incentives in the form of wage subsidies for the employment of older people.

- Rehabilitation programmes aimed at maintaining the working lives of older people, including health promotion projects in the workplace.

Fundamental to any approach, however, must be more effective training for people experiencing a number of moves in and out of the workforce. The evidence so far suggests that workers still do not have enough access to training, and this may be a particular problem for women workers – the group most affected by changes to the labour market. Table 2.5 illustrates this point using data from Wave 1 of the British Household Panel Survey*. The survey had a number of

---

* Table 2.5 uses material from Wave 1 of the British Household Panel Survey (BHPS), a national household panel survey of more than 10,000 individuals in some 5,500 households in Britain. The sample was drawn from the small users file of the Postcode Address File and covers non-institutional residences in England, Wales and Scotland. The BHPS is an annual survey which started in September 1991 and will return to re-interview members on an annual basis over the coming years.

Table 2.5 Training in current job of baby boomers (1991) (percentages)

		Aged 20–31		Aged 43–45	
		M	*W*	*M*	*W*
Induction training	Yes	46	46	32	31
	No	54	54	68	69
Training to improve skills	Yes	76	82	72	78
	No	25	20	28	22
Increase skills (eg by	Yes	64	57	63	57
learning new technology)	No	36	43	37	43
Preparation for future jobs	Yes	60	50	44	47
	No	40	50	56	52
Develop skills generally	Yes	77	76	70	67
	No	22	24	30	33

M, men (n = 463); W, women (n = 451)

Source: British Household Panel Survey, Wave 1.

questions concerned with training, and the answers have been linked with our two baby boom generations. Significant minorities (and majorities in some cases) are still receiving very limited job-related training of the type that might be expected (and which is almost certainly desirable). For example, most women are still not being prepared for future jobs, despite the fact that – and especially in the case of the second baby boom generation – the experience of constant changes in job and work status is inevitable. Moreover, significant numbers of women are not being given the opportunity to increase their skills (eg by learning new technology), a fact that will clearly hamper their movement through the labour market later in their working lives.

These points demonstrate the continuing failure by government and employers to acknowledge the radical change to the life course that is transforming the lives of the baby boomers. From the certainty of the traditional life course built around defined periods of education, work and retirement, we have moved towards what has been labelled the post-modern life course. Moody (1993) has argued that the post-modern life course is essentially an extension of the norm of middle age in two directions: downward ('the disappearance of child-hood') and upward ('the third age'). In general terms, this suggests that an employment and training strategy should be equipping people for continual change and movement in terms of job and work status, with the possibility of new types of work attachments being developed as people move into the period of 'third age work'.

In more specific terms, activities in work and training over the next decade are likely to focus on recruitment, career progression and career exit. Some of the key issues in each of these areas are reviewed below, together with some policy proposals targeted at the two baby boom cohorts.

▪ Recruiting older workers

In terms of recruitment, current policies from both government and organisations such as the Institute of Personnel Management (IPM) argue that age should not be used as a primary discriminator and that employers should recognise the benefits of recruiting more mature and experienced applicants. Research suggests, however, that discrimination at the point of recruitment is still common. A study by Taylor and Walker (1994) found that 43 per cent of the employers they surveyed felt that age was an important issue in the recruitment of staff. The extent of age discrimination in advertising has also been documented in a variety of research studies (Naylor 1990; Laczko and Phillipson 1991; McGoldrick and Arrowsmith 1993).

Given this background, a number of initiatives are needed to help stimulate employment among both baby boom generations as they enter their early and middle working years. Possible strategies include the following:

▪ Targeting recruitment to diverse groups of mature and older workers, including those changing career in mid-life, displaced workers below state pension age, and early retirees.

▪ Marketing jobs to mature and older workers, tailoring messages to target groups and selecting the communication channels most likely to attract them.

- Focusing on the employment needs of women, with a major emphasis on greater public investment in the provision of childcare.

- Acknowledging the importance of other social groups, for example those from ethnic minorities, where the combined effect of discrimination on the grounds of age and ethnicity drastically limits employment prospects.

- Developing a broader range of social provision to support employees, greater recognition of the workplace needs of carers being one element of this (Corti, Lauire and Dex, 1994; Phillips, 1995).

■ Career progression for older workers

A variety of factors may either encourage or inhibit the progress of an individual through an organisation. Existing research suggests that older workers may encounter significant barriers, for example in areas such as training and career development. A survey by Re-Action Trust (1992) of 2000 employing organisations found that, although steps were being taken to remove age criteria in job advertising, there was less progress in respect of retraining and development for older and mature staff. Similar findings were reported in a survey by Coopers and Lybrand (1992). A survey of local authorities found that most (206, or 92 per cent) reported that older workers had the 'same opportunity as younger workers with regard to promotion and participation in training schemes'. On the other hand, there was only limited evidence from the survey that mature and older workers were being targeted with specialised training to provide them with new skills (Itzin and Phillipson, 1993).

Possible strategies for improving career development for older workers are likely to include:

- Developing effective training programmes targeted at different groups of workers to take account of variations in learning styles and levels of confidence.

- Developing a human resources planning and management policy tailored to the needs of an ageing workforce.

- Conducting annual age audits within the workplace. (An age audit is an analysis of the ages of the workforce within a company or organisation, the purpose being to examine its policies and procedures and to determine whether older workers have equal access to recruitment, training, promotion and other work activities.)

- Developing age awareness programmes for line managers to increase knowledge about age barriers within organisations.

- Introducing sabbatical leave as a right for all employees – manual as well as non-manual.

▪ Career exit

For the baby boomers, greater emphasis is likely to be placed on retirement planning, in terms of both financial provision and post-retirement lifestyles. In contrast to previous generations of retirees who received little in the way of pre-retirement provision (Phillipson and Strang, 1983), baby boomers are likely to demand far greater attention to what they will see as a major period of their life course. Some key policies that will need to be implemented include:

- Planning and developing strategies for the effective retirement – or career exit – of employees as thoroughly as for recruitment.

- Considering the possibilities of implementing:
  - phased retirement;
  - pre-retirement education;
  - exploring with the retiree future work options;
  - flexible retirement;
  - successor training;
  - special projects.

- Implementing a programme of pre-retirement education using counselling, life-planning and a variety of teaching and learning methods, as well as providing information on future voluntary and paid employment options, health, leisure, welfare and benefits.

- Developing mid-life planning courses to look at career development and alternative career needs.

Conclusion

The aim of all the policies identified must be to achieve the integration of older workers into society, either maintaining them in the workplace or facilitating options that develop new social roles, which may or may not have a work element. The reality so far has been that older workers have been poorly served by social and employment policies. The last two decades have seen a massive shake-out of second and third age workers. Many have, in consequence, been forced into a period of limbo in terms of their economic and social status. It is likely that the baby boomers will have greater expectations both about the nature of appropriate employment and about suitable lifestyles in retirement. In the field of employment and training, organisations will need to accept more responsibility for the management of change through the life course. The pressure for greater flexibility in work patterns has been a key feature over the past decade (Hewitt, 1993). Workers (and their families) are having to adjust to new ways of working, with the growth of part-time work, self-employment and related developments.

The likelihood is that virtually all the baby boomers will have experienced flexible working – and possibly most of them in the years just before retirement. This development will mean that employers must ensure that recruitment and career development strategies do not discriminate against mature workers as they move in and out of the workforce, in different types of jobs and at different levels of seniority. Governments must also take greater responsibility in developing the potential of an ageing workforce, a task that has been neglected over the past few years. If this neglect were to continue, however, serious questions would be raised about the waste for society at large of ignoring the abilities of mature and older people. The message of this chapter is that we need to develop new employment and training policies now, in the hope of securing significant change for those retiring in the years ahead.

■ Summary

- Post-war industrial change has resulted in major changes in the labour market – most notably the growth of 'flexible working', the decline of the manufacturing industry and the expansion in part-time working and self-employment.

- The 'traditional' life course with defined periods of education, work and retirement is being replaced by one in which there is significantly more fluidity and movement between statuses, especially in the labour market.

- The notion of a lifelong career has all but disappeared. Rather, temporary and transitional jobs may become a permanent feature of the employment experiences of the second baby boomers.

- More of second baby boom women work than previous generations. But most of this growth has been in part-time work and is concentrated in 'irregular' jobs providing 'discontinuous' employment.

- In the twenty-first century Britain may face a skills shortage as the number of younger workers diminishes. At the same time there will be more older workers (aged 50-plus) than ever before, and these workers will have higher expectations regarding their right to equal opportunities and to age 'productively'.

- Given changes in the labour market, we will require an employment and training strategy that will equip people for continual change and movement in terms of job and work status and will encourage the recruitment and retention of older workers.

3 Financial resources in later life

Ruth Hancock

Rising real earnings, increased occupational pension coverage, greater numbers of women in the workforce, the advent of personal pensions and more home ownership might all suggest that the baby boomers can look forward to a financially secure retirement. But the 1980s saw widening gaps between the incomes of those on high and low earnings; and between those in work and those without a job (see, for example, Goodman and Webb, 1994; Gosling, Machin and Meghir, 1994). Moreover, as Chapter 2 discusses, changes in the labour market have resulted in less secure employment for those in work, with more temporary jobs and fixed-term employment contracts. The proportion of employees belonging to an employer-run pension scheme has now stabilised. Given the close dependence of income in retirement on lifetime work histories, earnings levels and pension scheme membership, any complacency about the financial status of the baby boomers in retirement is premature. The size of the baby boom cohorts in relation to the numbers in subsequent generations who will be producing the goods and services the baby boomers need in retirement will be a further source of pressure on baby boomers' retirement incomes. A closer look at what we know – and cannot yet know – about the influences on their future incomes is justified.

This chapter reviews provision for retirement as it affects the baby boom generations, examines the working lives of baby boomers and how these are likely to affect their financial resources in retirement, and looks briefly at the effects of more widespread home ownership. This is followed by discussion of recent trends in the incomes of today's pensioners and policy issues for the future.

■ Provision for retirement

The first baby boom coincided with the birth of a new system of state pensions in the UK. With its roots in the Beveridge Report (Beveridge, 1942), the system comprised a flat rate payable to everyone with sufficient contributions, irrespective of other resources. Around the time of the second baby boom, a supplementary system of earnings-related ('graduated') pensions was introduced. Just as the second generation of baby boomers were beginning their careers, this rather modest system of earnings-related pensions was replaced by a more generous State Earnings Related Pension Scheme (SERPS), which would have been fully mature well before the first generation of baby boomers reached retirement. In recent years concern about the future costs of pensions for growing numbers of pensioners, when the working age population is shrinking (see Chapter 1, Figure 1.3), has been behind various measures designed to reduce the burden on the public purse and to encourage more personal provision for retirement.

To reduce the cost of state pensions, SERPS has been reduced significantly in scope (by the 1986 Social Security Act and the 1995 Pensions Act); throughout the 1980s the basic state pension has been indexed to price inflation rather than earnings, so it is now worth around 15 per cent of average earnings compared with 20 per cent in 1979 (Johnson, Disney and Stears, 1996); incentives to opt out of SERPS through private pensions have been increased. The government's decision to equalise state pension ages for men and women at 65 was justified largely on grounds of affordability (Department of Social Security, 1993). The levels of Income Support (the main form of means-tested social assistance in the UK) for pensioners are now above the level of the basic state pension. Any pensioner with only the basic state pension is therefore entitled to a means-tested supplement. However, not all changes in the life of baby boomers have been designed to reduce public spending on state pensions. The introduction of 'Home Responsibilities Protection' means that rights to the basic state pension, and in future SERPS, are protected to some extent against periods spent out of the labour force bringing up children or looking after a disabled or elderly relative. The removal of the 'earnings rule' means that any post-retirement earnings no longer reduce the state pension.

Since the birth of the first baby boomers, the proportion of employees belonging to an employer's pension scheme has risen from 28 per cent in 1953 to a peak of 53 per cent in 1967 (Government Actuary's Department (GAD), 1994) and has stabilised at about 50 per cent since then. The experiences of men and women have been different. The proportion of women employees belonging to an employer's pension scheme increased substantially, from 21 per cent in 1963 to 37 per cent twenty years later. The percentage of male employees belonging to an employer's scheme peaked at two-thirds in 1967; in 1991, at just 57 per cent, it was lower than at any time for about thirty years.

The experiences of different cohorts are contrasted in Figure 3.1, in which rates of membership in occupational schemes at selected ages

Figure 3.1 Membership of occupational pension schemes (a) at age 43–47 years and (b) at age 27–33 years, by gender and birth cohort

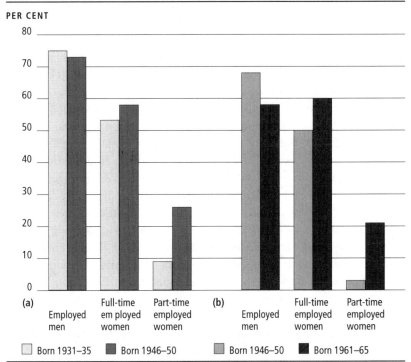

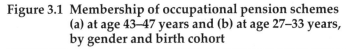

Source: 1978 and 1993 General Household Surveys, reported in Evandrou and Falkingham (1997).

are plotted. Figure 3.1a shows that the proportion of employed men from the first baby boom cohort who were members of an occupational pension scheme when they were in their mid-40s (43–47 years) was just a little lower (73 per cent) than that for men from the generation born fifteen years earlier (75 per cent). However, comparing the first and second baby boom cohorts (Figure 3.1b), the proportion of employed men who were in pension schemes around the age of 30 years was distinctly lower for the second (58 per cent) than for the first baby boomers (68 per cent). The detrimental effect of this lower rate on the future pensions of men from the later baby boom cohort is compounded by the fact that, at this age, lower proportions of second baby boom men were in employment at all, compared with the first cohort (Evandrou and Falkingham, 1997).

The trend is different for women, occupational pension coverage being higher at each age for each subsequent generation. For the second baby boomers, slightly more women than men, working full-time, were covered by occupational pension schemes at the age of 27–33 years. The increase in coverage for women working part-time is also striking, although the figures among part-time employees remains well below that for full-time employees. Together with greater participation in the labour force, these increased rates of pension coverage suggest that women from the baby boom generations will be more likely than their predecessors to have some income from an occupational pension of their own. Because of their greater propensity to work part-time, however, the proportion with an occupational pension is still likely to be below that for men. Moreover, the size of their pensions may be quite small.

Until 1988, only employer-run pension schemes, whose benefits were defined in relation to years of service and salary levels ('defined benefit' schemes), could be used to contract out of SERPS. In 1988, it became possible to use 'defined contribution' schemes in general, and *personal* pensions in particular, as an alternative to SERPS. Under such schemes, the pension that is payable on retirement depends on rates of return earned on the contributions paid into a fund and on annuity rates when the fund is converted to an annuity. Some of the decline in membership in an occupational pension scheme must be explained by a switch to personal pensions. The number of people with personal pensions has risen from under 2 million in 1987/8 to more than 5.5 million in 1992/3 (Department of Social Security, 1995a). In 1994, 28 per cent of men employed full-time had a personal pension, as did 20 per cent of women employed full-time and 11 per cent of women employed part-time (OPCS, 1996). Growth in personal pensions has been particularly strong for people in their early 30s. The proportion of employees belonging to personal pension schemes was highest (36 per cent for men and 24 per cent for women employed full-time) in the age group 25–34, which contains the second baby boomers. Corresponding figures for the first baby boomers were 25 per cent (men) and 18 per cent (women employed full-time).

It is too early to judge what will be the implications of this shift towards personal pensions – a shift that will be felt more by the second than the first generation of baby boomers. All pension schemes are subject to some risks. An individual's personal pension, however, depends directly on the performance of his or her individual fund and on the annuity rates on offer when the pension is purchased. Even if personal pension funds perform well on average (and this will depend largely on the performance of the economy), there will probably be considerable variation and some will perform badly. If nothing else, the switch to personal pensions may thus contribute to greater inequality in the retirement incomes of the baby boomers. There is now considerable evidence that many of those who have withdrawn from an employer pension in favour of a personal pension would have done better to stay with their employer's scheme. In addition, many people contribute only small amounts to personal pensions and in the long run much will depend on their ability to sustain adequate contributions over their working lives.

▪ The working lives of the baby boomers

Levels of state and employer pensions payable on retirement depend directly on lifetime patterns of work and earnings. The rights accumulated under a personal pension depend on how much has been contributed to the fund, for how long funds have been accumulating interest and the rates of return earned on the fund. The first two of these are also likely to depend on lifetime patterns of earnings because they determine what level of contributions into the fund can be afforded and what level is allowed (there are legal limits, dependent on age and earnings, on annual contributions to a pension). The ability to save in other forms is also influenced by lifetime income levels.

Interruptions to employment through unemployment and the demands of bringing up children, caring for elderly relatives and so forth are thus detrimental to the accumulation of pension rights and the ability to save in other ways. So, too, are part-time working compared with full-time working and persistently low earnings. Today 44 per cent of women get a state retirement pension that is below the full basic state pension level for a single person, either because they have paid insufficient contributions in their own right or because they receive a reduced pension on their husband's contribution (Department of Social Security, 1995). For men the proportion is much lower – just over 5 per cent – but is none the less at historically high levels (*Hansard*, 1995). In his latest projections (GAD, 1995), the Government Actuary assumes that over 90 per cent of women from the first baby boom, and all from the second, will retire with some entitlement to a basic state pension in their own right. However, around 20 per cent of women from the first baby boom will be entitled to less than a full pension, although for women retiring in 2020/1, a little before the second baby boomers retire, the proportion not entitled to a full pension is expected to have fallen to 9 per cent. Patchy work records seem set to continue to reduce the entitlement to state pensions of many women and a small minority of men. Given that protection against unemployment and family responsibilities is virtually non-existent for private sector pensions, the effects on occupational and personal pensions must be greater still.

Men's working lives have been getting shorter as a consequence of later school-leaving and earlier retirement. Both these trends are assumed to continue, at least until 2006, in the latest official projections of future rates of economic activity (Employment Department, 1996). Using a representative sample* of work histories of men and

---

* Derived from the 1988 Retirement Survey (RS) (see Bone et al, 1992) and surveys conducted in 1986 and 1987 under the ESRC's Social Change and Economic Life Initiative (SCELI). Hancock et al (1995) gives further details.

women aged between 20 and 69 in the middle to late 1980s, it is possible to compare the accumulated years of paid work, at selected ages, for individuals belonging to different birth cohorts. This is what is demonstrated in Figure 3.2, in which the median accumulated years in full-time employment by age 35 is shown for men and women born between 1921 and 1950. The last of these, people born from 1946 to 1950, the first wave of baby boomers. For men the median accumulated years in full-time employment by the age of 35 has fallen from 20.1 years for the cohort born 1921–25 (most of whom left school before the age of 15) to 17.8 for members of the first baby boom. For women there has also been a decline, from 9.8 years to 7.8 years, despite the increase in their participation in the labour force. As Chris Phillipson shows in Chapter 2, much of the increase in participation in paid work among women has been in part-time employment. Equivalent comparisons in accumulated years of part-time employment between younger and older cohorts do show an increase, although by the second half of the 1980s this was discernible only for women who

Figure 3.2 Median accumulated work experience at age 35, by gender and birth cohort

Source: analysis of RS (1988) and SCELI surveys (1986–87).

had reached the age of 40 (Hancock, Jarvis and Mueller, 1995), which does not include the second baby boom cohort.

An idea of the outlook for the pension entitlements of women of the first baby boom can be obtained from Figure 3.3. This plots the median accumulated years of work experience (full- and part-time employment and self-employment) of men and women of the first baby boom and of their counterparts born twenty years earlier. For the older of these two generations we can see how work experience accumulated up to the age of 55. The comparison between men and women is striking. Men's work experience increased more or less in proportion to age. The median number of years of work experience was lower for women than for men even at the age of 25, and

Figure 3.3 Median number of years in paid work at selected ages; selected birth cohorts, by gender

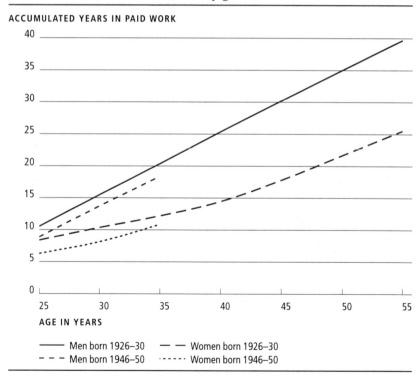

ACCUMULATED YEARS IN PAID WORK

AGE IN YEARS

——— Men born 1926–30   — — Women born 1926–30
– – – Men born 1946–50   ····· Women born 1946–50

Source: analysis of RS (1988) and SCELI surveys (1986–87).

thereafter the gap widened. The effect of later school-leaving is evident for both men and women in the first baby boom cohort. The difference between men and women is just as obvious as for the earlier generation, although the beginnings of an upturn for women of the baby boom cohort compared with the earlier cohort is apparent by the age of 35, and it seems reasonable to assume that by older ages the baby boomer women will have acquired more years' work experience than the older generation. Even so, on present experience much of it will be part-time. The prospects of their catching up with men by the time they retire are very remote.

Tables 3.1 and 3.2 summarise the work histories of the 1940s baby boomers and of earlier generations at the age of 35 (the mid-1980s for the first baby boomers). For men, the experiences of the baby boomers differ from previous cohorts in a number of ways that could be

Table 3.1 Summary of men's work histories to age 35 by birth cohort

	Men born:					
	1921–25	1926–30	1931–35	1936–40	1941–45	1946–50
Full-time employment						
Accumulated employment experience – median (years)	20.1	20.0	19.2	18.8	18.1	17.8
Job duration – average (years)	3.6	3.7	3.6	3.9	3.7	3.3
Job duration – upper quartile (years)	4.8	4.5	4.8	5.1	5.0	4.3
Unemployment						
Ever experienced (%)	15	15	10	10	15	25
Spell duration – median (months)	3	3	4	5	4	5
Spell duration – upper quartile (months)	11	8	14	11	6	12
Part-time employment – ever experienced (%)	1.3	1.0	2.3	2.4	4.5	2.7
Self-employment – ever experienced	12	11	9	9	18	17

Source: analysis of RS (1988) and SCELI surveys (1986–87).

Table 3.2 Summary of women's work histories to age 35 by birth cohort

	Women born:					
	1921– 25	1926– 30	1931– 35	1936– 40	1941– 45	1946 50
Full-time employment						
Accumulated employment experience: median (years)	9.8	10.2	9.5	8.7	8.1	7.8
upper quartile (years)	13.8	14.8	13.3	12.1	11.3	10.8
Part-time employment						
Ever experienced (%)	29	31	39	44	58	58
Accumulated employment experience: average (years)	1.0	1.1	1.4	1.5	2.5	2.2
upper quartile (years)	0.4	0.8	1.7	2.2	4.4	3.8
Self-employment - ever experienced (%)	3	3	4	8	5	7

Source: analysis of RS (1988) and SCELI surveys (1986–87).

detrimental to their incomes in retirement. Some of these changes represent a halting or reversal of a trend. An example is job duration. Future rights to occupational pensions are generally affected adversely by job changes, and many occupational pension schemes require members to have worked for their employer for a minimum period. For earlier generations, job durations were growing but this trend was reversed for baby boomers. To take another example, the proportion of baby boomers who had experienced unemployment by the age of 35 was very much higher than for any previous generation. The proportion of men who had experienced part-time working was low among all cohorts, but an upward trend across cohorts was halted for the baby boomers. The baby boomers and the five-year cohort immediately preceding them were more likely than any previous generation to have experienced self-employment by the age of 35. Self-employment brings no rights to SERPS, and self-employed people must make their own arrangements for a personal pension if they are to have more than the basic state pension when they retire.

For women the most striking trend across cohorts is the rise in the proportion who had ever experienced part-time employment by the age of 35: from 28 per cent of women born in the first half of the 1920s to 58 per cent of the first baby boomers. Part-time jobs are much less likely than full-time jobs to provide an employer's pension and far more likely to pay earnings below the limit at which National Insurance contributions become payable. Rights to a state pension are therefore less likely to be earned through part-time work.

▪ Home ownership and housing inheritance as financial resources in later life

Although recurrent income, dominated by state and private pensions, is likely to remain the chief financial resource for people in retirement, a growing proportion of retired people are home owners and have a potentially valuable asset in the form of the equity tied up in their homes. Increasing numbers have also acquired other forms of financial wealth. Apart from any desire to leave bequests on death, later life is a time when one might reasonably choose to run down wealth to obtain a higher standard of living than income alone affords.

Figure 3.4 plots the proportion of people who owned* their own homes in 1993 by age group. The age group 46–50 corresponds to the first wave of baby boomers. At almost 80 per cent, the proportion who are owners is higher than for any other age group. This is the outcome of a number of factors. The long-term increase in the proportions of successive cohorts who ever became owner-occupiers, typically in their late 20s and 30s, explains why owner-occupation is currently lowest among the oldest cohorts. Secondly, the sale of council houses in the 1980s to sitting tenants gave a boost to owner-occupation among those in their 40s and 50s. In general, once people have bought their first homes they remain in the owner-occupied sector for the rest of their lives, unless they move to live with relatives or into a residential setting in very old age. Recent increases in mortgage arrears and consequent repossessions and more family breakdowns counteract this general tendency to some extent. Nevertheless, it seems likely that

---

* Home owners are defined here as heads of households and their partners (married or unmarried) living in owner-occupied housing. As elsewhere in this chapter, the non-household population is excluded from the analysis.

Figure 3.4 Owner-occupation rates by age groups; UK, 1993

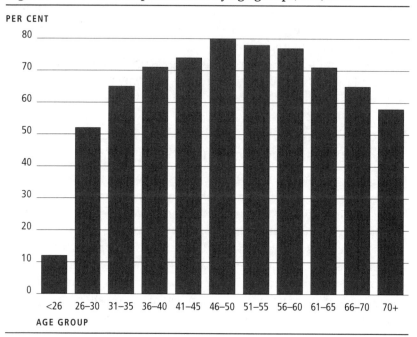

PER CENT

AGE GROUP

Source: FES 1993, analysed by the Gerontology Data Service.

between three-quarters and four-fifths of the first baby boomers will enter retirement owning their own homes.

Suggestions that current and future generations of older owner-occupiers can release significant amounts of equity from their homes have been tempered by a number of recent studies (eg Mullings and Hamnett, 1992; Gibbs and Oldman, 1993; Rolfe, Leather and Mackintosh, 1993). Recent projections also point to an increase in the proportion of older owner-occupiers who are still paying off a mortgage (Holmans and Frosztega, 1994). By 2011, the proportion of owner-occupiers aged 65–74 (containing the first baby boomers) who will still have a mortgage has been put at 29 per cent compared with 13 per cent for the corresponding age group in 1991. Of owners aged 45–64 in 2011 (including the second baby boomers), 77 per cent are expected to still have a mortgage, compared with 61 per cent of their counterparts in 1991 (Holmans and Frosztega, 1994). Nevertheless, the scope for housing equity to boost income in retirement remains, and new equity release schemes are coming on to the market, which could help.

If the scope for releasing home equity is less than has sometimes been suggested, what of the effect of increased home ownership on inheritances, which might also boost the resources of future cohorts of pensioners? Table 3.3 presents estimates and projections of the proportions of people who had, or will have, inherited house (or flat) property at selected ages for 1989/90 and 2011. The older two ages (60 and 65) correspond approximately to the ages of the first baby boomers in 2011, and the younger ages to the ages of the second baby boomers in 2011. Compared with their counterparts in 1989/90, considerably greater proportions are projected to have inherited house (or flat) property by this time in their lives. Between 35 and 40 per cent of the first baby boomers might be expected to have inherited some house (or flat) property as they enter retirement; 20–25 per cent of the second baby boomers may have done so by their late 40s. However, the sizes of such inheritances are not projected to change very much in real terms from their 1989/90 levels, when a third were less than £10,000 and under a fifth were more than £50,000. In terms of generating an income (or meeting the costs of care in old age) these sums are not large.

Table 3.3 Projections of cumulative percentages of people who will have inherited housing wealth by successive ages (%)

BY AGE:	1989/90	2011
45 years	14	20
50 years	18	26
60 years	26	36
65 years	27	38

Source: Holmans and Frosztega (1994, Tables K.3 and K.4).

■ Recent trends in pensioners' incomes

Pensioners' incomes are considerably higher on average than in the past, leading some to conclude that poverty in old age is no longer a primary concern. Yet we have seen from the work histories and pension records of members of the baby boom cohorts that inadequate incomes in retirement cannot be ruled out. A growing gap between rich and poor pensioners emerged in the 1980s (Hancock and Weir, 1994) and pensioners are still among the poorer groups in the population (Goodman and Webb, 1994). The growing contrast between the incomes of rich and poor pensioners has its roots in the changed contributions of different sources of income in retirement, changes that have not been universal.

The principal sources of pensioners' incomes are private pensions (employer-run schemes and personal pension plans), investments, earnings and state benefits. The last of these include the state retirement pension, means-tested benefits (Income Support, Housing Benefit and Council Tax Benefit or its forerunner Community Charge Benefit) and other state benefits (eg War Pension, Attendance Allowance).

Private pension income

In 1979 just under two-fifths of pensioner units* had some income from an occupational pension. By 1990 this proportion had grown to three-fifths but since then there has been no further increase. Moreover, the percentage of recently retired pensioners with an occupational pension has *declined* slightly: from 69 per cent in 1990/1 to 66 per cent in 1993 (Department of Social Security, 1995b). Already the levelling-off of occupational pension coverage has had consequences for the current generation of pensioners.

At the same time that the proportion of pensioners with occupational pensions has been increasing, so too have the amounts they receive. The average for all those with any occupational pension rose by 63 per cent in the fourteen years to 1993; between 1990/1 and 1993

---

* Single people who have reached state pension age and couples in which the husband is aged 65 or over.

alone it increased by 10 per cent to stand at £74 per week in July 1993 prices (Department of Social Security, 1995b). However, the *average* occupational pension overstates the amounts received by most occupational pensioners, because it is affected by relatively small numbers with very large occupational pensions. The *median* occupational pension income, among those with any such income, is typically not much more than half the average level. For example, in 1993, when the average level was £74, the median was £39. These figures are based on pensioner *units*: single people over state pension age and couples where the husband is over state pension age. When *individual* pensioner incomes are examined, some important differences are exposed.

Women are much less likely than men to have income from an occupational pension. In 1993, two-thirds of men aged 65–74 had an occupational pension and the amount men received averaged £87 a week. The proportion of women aged 60–74 with an occupational pension (whether in their own right or via their husband) was just a third and its average level was £42 (Family Expenditure Survey (FES), 1993, analysis conducted through the Gerontology Data Service (GDS)). Differences between the incomes of individual older and younger pensioners were less than between men and women. Over the age of 75, 65 per cent of men had an occupational pension that averaged £73 a week compared with 30 per cent of women with an average pension of £43. For women marital status is significant. Never-married women are the most likely to be receiving an occupational pension and tend to receive larger pensions than other women (Table 3.4). Widows are more likely than married women to receive some occupational pension. This is because they inherit their husbands' pensions. Married women are the least likely to be receiving an occupational pension; relatively few of them have earned a pension in their own right. Even with greater numbers of women receiving an occupational pension, it seems likely that these differences will also be apparent for the baby boom women.

Currently about 2 per cent of women receive income from a personal pension or their forerunners (retirement annuities) compared with 7 per cent of men. The amounts of personal pensions in payment are much larger among younger men than they are for older men. On average, men aged 65–74 who are in receipt of a personal pension or

Table 3.4 Receipt of income from an occupational pension, women in the UK aged 60+, by marital status, 1991–1993

	Percentage with any occupational pension	Sample size	For those with any occupational pension		
			Mean (£ pw)*	Median (£ pw)*	Sample size
Aged 60–74					
Married	21	2,394	33.70	23.30	508
Widowed	53	1,125	34.40	23.30	593
Never married	62	234	62.60	50.90	146
Divorced/separated	27	215	36.10	30.50	58
Aged 75 and over					
Married	10	500	34.30	15.20	52
Widowed	38	1,225	34.80	20.10	460
Never married	44	171	63.50	53.30	76
Divorced/separated	16	49	–	–	8

*1993 prices

Source: 1991–93 Family Expenditure Survey, analysed through the GDS.

retirement annuity received £82 a week compared with £39 received by older men. The median amount for older men was just £9 compared with £28 for younger men. Amounts received by women are smaller and there is less difference between older and younger women, averaging about £20 a week (FES 1993, analysis through the GDS). With the growth of personal pensions, we would expect rather greater proportions of baby boomers – especially those from the second baby boom – to be receiving an income from a personal pension. Whether the amounts they receive are much larger, and whether they supplement or replace other sources of pensions, remains to be seen.

Investment income

The ten years from 1979 to 1989 also saw an increase from three-fifths to three-quarters in the proportion of pensioner units with some income from investments (Hancock and Weir, 1994; Department of Social Security, 1995a). In 1993 the proportion stood at 73 per cent

(Department of Social Security, 1995b). Average amounts have also increased but the contrast between average and median amounts is even more striking than for occupational pensions, indicating that many pensioners have very low levels of savings/investment income: the average investment income (among pensioners with any such income) of £37 a week compared with a median level of £9. The prospects for the baby boom cohorts are mixed. Growth in share ownership, for example, might mean greater access to savings in retirement. However, high rates of borrowing in the late 1980s and the resulting increase in indebtedness, exacerbated by the housing market slump, might mean the reverse. Dependence on savings income in retirement also implies vulnerability to volatile interest rates. Interest rate cuts, welcomed by younger people with mortgages, are much less welcome to pensioners.

Earnings

Earnings are now a less common source of income in retirement than they used to be, despite the abolition of the earnings rule, the fact that those over state pension age are not required to pay National Insurance contributions and also have higher tax allowances than younger people – all of which enhance the reward from working beyond state pension age. In 1971, 30 per cent of men aged 65–69 and 11 per cent aged over 70 were economically active (in a job or looking for one). By 1994 these proportions had halved (Employment Department, 1996). Although more women have jobs, the proportion of those economically active over state pension age has also fallen. In 1991, 8 per cent of women aged 65–69 and 2 per cent of those aged 70–74 were in paid work either as an employee or self-employed (Jarvis et al, 1996). These relatively low rates of participation in paid work were reflected in the contribution of earnings to total income. On average, income from employment or self-employment contributed just 7 per cent of the personal income of men in their first five years after reaching state pension age, 3 per cent for those aged 70–74 and just 1 per cent for those aged 75 years and over. The role of earnings in women's incomes was smaller still, the corresponding proportions being 3 per cent, 1 per cent and 0.1 per cent. However, for pensioner units who received income from earnings, the value of that income increased by 37 per cent in real terms over the period 1979–89 (Hancock and Weir, 1994). Earnings could become a more important source of income for pensioners from the baby boom generations if the demand for their labour increases as the ratio of workers to pensioners decreases. But early retirement continues to be a desire of many people, although substantial proportions expect to do some work after retiring (Hancock, Jarvis and Mueller, 1995).

State benefits

Despite the changes mentioned above, state benefits (including the state retirement pension) continue to be the main source of pensioners' income. Virtually all receive some income from the state. In 1993, 53 per cent of all pensioner income came from state benefits (Department of Social Security, 1995b). This is almost the same as in 1970, more than twenty years earlier (Dawson and Evans, 1987). However, it is less than in the more recent past. The contribution of state benefits to pensioner income peaked at 64 per cent in 1982. More than 30 per cent of pensioners now receive means-tested benefits of one form or another (Retirement Income Inquiry, 1996) and more are entitled to such benefits but do not claim them (Department of Social Security, 1995c).

Trends in the contribution of the main sources of pensioners' income are illustrated in Figure 3.5. In summary, more pensioners now have some income from private pensions and savings but in many cases the amounts are quite small. State benefits in general, and the basic state pension in particular (Hancock and Weir, 1994), remain the major source of income for many pensioners. Earnings contribute much less to incomes in retirement than they use to, although those who do have some earnings earn considerably more in retirement than their counterparts ten or more years ago.

Figure 3.5 Sources of pensioner incomes, 1970–93

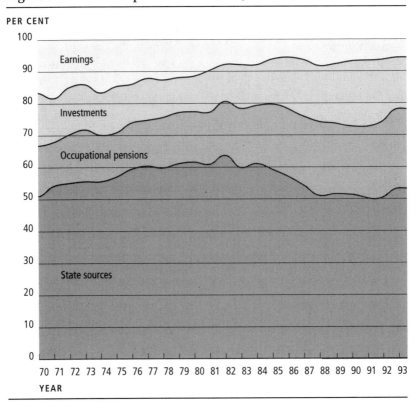

PER CENT

Source: Dawson and Evans (1987); Department of Social Security (1995b).

Total income

Long-term changes in total pensioner income are summarised in Table 3.5. The 1960s was a decade in which pensioner incomes became more equal. The incomes of those in the lowest fifth (quintile) of the income distribution were 41 per cent higher in 1971/2 than ten years earlier, compared with 11 per cent for those in the highest fifth. On average, pensioner incomes rose by less than those of non-pensioners (11 per cent compared with 19 per cent). The next decade saw a continuation of this trend, the incomes of the poorest fifth of pensioners growing by 38 per cent compared with 22 per cent for the richest fifth of pensioners. Over this period, the income of pensioners rose, on average, by double the increase in average income of non-pensioners. The 1980s saw an increase in average pensioner income of 38 per cent – much larger than either of the previous two decades and on a par with the increase for non-pensioners. However, the incomes of the poorest pensioner rose by just 10 per cent compared with 57 per cent for the richest.

Table 3.5 Changes in equivalent pensioner unit incomes, 1961–91

	Average pensioner income	Median pensioner income			Average non-pensioner income
		Lowest quintile	Middle quintile	Highest quintile	
1961(/2) to 1971(/2)	+11%	+41%	+30%	+11%	+19%
1971(/2) to 1981(/2)	+25%	+38%	+30%	+22%	+12%
1981(/2) to 1991(/2)	+38%	+10%	+26%	+57%	+39%

Source: Goodman and Webb (1994, Figure 3.13); Johnson et al (1996, Table 3.3).

▪ Policy issues

Under present pension arrangements and trends in lifetime employment, income inequality seems likely to feature strongly in the financial circumstances of pensioners from the baby boom cohorts. Income inequality does not necessarily mean poverty, but pension rights and other forms of wealth accumulated during working lives seem unlikely to be sufficient to prevent some people from experiencing poverty in old age, while for other baby boomers retirement will be a time of relative affluence.

When the ratio of workers to retired people is declining (see Chapter 1, Figure 1.3), larger transfers of goods and services between the two groups – by whatever mechanisms – are unavoidable if the living standards of retired people are to be protected. Policies aimed at tempering the decline in this ratio are the only way to reduce the scale of these transfers. As Chris Phillipson advocates in Chapter 2, making sure that we take advantage of the willingness and ability of older people to contribute to production (ie to work) is clearly a sensible approach. Recognising (and quantifying) the unpaid but productive contributions of older people, for example as carers and volunteers (see Chapter 6), is also important when gauging the true extent of net transfers from 'productive' to 'non-productive' members of society. But neither removes altogether the potential problems of an ageing population.

So the next questions that must be asked are: How big are these problems? How significant a problem will the future financing of pensions be? A number of recent studies have argued that, in the UK, the welfare state in general and state pensions in particular do not face insuperable funding crises (eg Hills, 1993; Hutton, Kennedy and Whiteford, 1995). Rising real incomes among those in work make greater transfers to pensioners less painful. Some increase in tax revenues will be generated automatically and some increase in tax rates or National Insurance contributions is likely to be more acceptable if the real incomes of those having to pay them are growing steadily. This does imply, however, that those in work need to be willing to see their net incomes rise less than their productivity and so share some of the benefits of productivity growth with pensioners. In fact, the Government Actuary (GAD, 1995) has estimated that, with the basic state pension indexed to price inflation and modest (1.5 per cent per annum) real earnings growth, the combined employer and employee class 1 National Insurance contribution rate needed to finance state pensions and other insurance benefits can fall from 18.25 per cent in 1994/5 to 14 per cent by 2050/1. By the time the first baby boomers are retiring, the National Insurance rate could be allowed to fall to around 17.5 per cent, and by the time the second baby boomers retire, the necessary rate would be only 14 per cent. However, the value of the basic state pension would have become 'nugatory'* (ie worthless) in relation to average earnings. Up-rating the basic state pension level each year from now by the increase in earnings would lead to a required National Insurance rate of over 25 per cent; but expressed support for increases in taxation to pay for more spending on the welfare state grew substantially during the 1980s (Askham, Hancock and

---

* In the words of Michael Portillo, then Chief Secretary to the Treasury, in a much-quoted article in *The Guardian*, 8 December 1993.

Hills, 1995; Hancock, Jarvis and Mueller, 1995). To retain acceptability, however, such policies are likely to depend on ever-increasing productivity (to pay for continued and widespread increases in real earnings) and low levels of unemployment. Many pension reforms have been suggested (Dilnot and Johnson, 1992; Falkingham and Johnson, 1993; Field and Owen, 1993; Atkinson, 1994; Townsend and Walker, 1995; Castle and Townsend, 1996; Lynes, 1996; Retirement Income Inquiry, 1996) and new variants are being proposed all the time, including recent Conservative Government proposals (Department of Social Security, 1997) to replace state pensions with personalised pension funds. Some proposals involve enhancing the existing state pay-as-you-go system under which today's workers pay for the pensions of today's pensioners, but most seem reluctant to advocate higher National Insurance contributions or taxes to finance better state pensions. Instead, they appear to assume that people are more willing to pay into a form of personalised savings account, or fund, to pay for their *own* old age than they are to pay taxes to contribute towards the pensions of other people. A move in this direction limits the scope for any redistribution of income from those who are well-off during their working lives to those who are not so well-off and less able to contribute to their own pension fund. The success of personalised funded schemes rests very much on these funds being able to earn good rates of return, something for which there is no guarantee.

Private provision for old age is frequently suggested as a solution to the problem of financing income in retirement. More private sector provision implies a reduced role for the state – which may be favoured on ideological grounds – and containment of public debt and/or taxation – which is argued to be necessary to promote economic growth. In practice, the relationship between public sector activity and economic performance is at best uncertain (Atkinson, 1995), and in relevant areas (eg some kinds of insurance, inflation-proofing pensions), state intervention can improve on the workings of the free market economy (see, for example, Barr, 1993). Even so, macro-economic considerations restrict the scope for significant increases in the ratio of public spending to national output.

Most proposals for more reliance on private sector pensions acknowledge its limitations (see, for example, World Bank, 1994).

Typically they expect the state to step in to cover periods when individuals cannot afford to contribute to a pension, and to assume ultimate responsibility for protecting the real value of pensions against inflation. In addition, some compulsion for everyone to make their own provision for retirement, combined with considerable regulation of private sector pension providers, is usually deemed necessary. The second generation of baby boomers in particular will have experienced more fragmented employment histories and different pension schemes from their predecessors. In retirement, the financial well-being of those who have fared worst from these changes will depend heavily on how far the state does step in where the private sector has not delivered an adequate pension.

A further line of reasoning is that private sector pensions are preferable to state pensions because they are funded rather than pay-as-you-go. In principle, there is no reason why state pensions cannot be funded, although any transition from a pay-as-you-go to a funded scheme faces considerable difficulties (Falkingham and Johnson, 1993). However, funded mechanisms do not remove the need for transfers from 'workers' to 'non-workers' (see, for example, Barr, 1992, 1993), although it is sometimes argued that they are better for the economy because they result in more saving and hence more investment. In general, however, any increase in savings is only while the fund is building up and it is questionable whether funded pension systems are any better at increasing the economy's overall productivity (Barr, 1992, 1993). They may, however, disguise the extent of transfers from workers to pensioners and therefore be more acceptable.

Pensioners will always have to compete with other groups not able to generate sufficient incomes through paid work. This would be the case even if their numbers were not growing. In view of the fact that some pensioners are considerably better off than their counterparts used to be, it may still be reasonable to ask whether some of the state support that goes to them might be better channelled elsewhere. A common response is to call for more 'targeting' in state support for older people to prevent resources being 'wasted' on older people who do not 'need' it. Dilnot and Johnson (1992), for example, showed the extent to which poorer pensioners are helped more, and richer ones less, by increasing the rates of Income Support rather than increasing the basic state pension.

Means-testing has substantial drawbacks, however. In the first place it will act as a disincentive to provide for one's own retirement – the so-called 'savings trap' – particularly for those able to earn only small private pensions or accumulate only modest savings, who may find themselves no better off in retirement than if they had not made any provision themselves. Secondly, means-tested benefits are subject to non-take-up, limiting their effectiveness in helping people in most need. If containment of costs of the state pension (and means-tested supplements to it) is one objective, there are alternatives such as a 'Minimum Pension Guarantee' (Atkinson, 1994; Commission on Social Justice, 1994) or an 'Assured Minimum Pension' (Retirement Income Inquiry, 1996). Such schemes involve some means-testing, usually of any pension income but not necessarily of other forms of income or wealth. They could also involve less frequent means-testing, the main test being on retirement. Such reforms also offer the possibility of addressing other problems with the current system: for example, if individual-based, they could ensure a minimum pension for all individuals so that it would be of particular help to women without much pension in their own right. Although the focus of much recent attention on pension reform has been the affordability of existing systems, especially state pensions, most recognise that there is more wrong with the present UK system than just its affordability.

Long-term care

Pension systems and income in retirement have been the focus of a great deal of attention for a number of years. More recently, concern has grown for another aspect of finances in later life: paying for long-term care. With more people living longer and fewer being cared for free of charge by the National Health Service when they become frail, more older people are having to face the substantial costs of paying for long-term care in a residential or nursing home, or indeed for care provided to them in their own homes. Existing pension systems have not been designed to achieve the level of income required to meet such costs. Whereas Income Support is available to those with the lowest incomes and levels of savings, many older people with relatively modest means are having to meet in full or make a contribution to the costs of any long-term care they need. This raises a new set of issues in relation to provision for retirement. To date, proposals to help individuals meet the cost of care have revolved around using the equity tied up in their homes and various forms of insurance policies.

▪ Conclusion

The prospect of the retirement of the large cohorts of baby boomers highlights the potential problems of retirement provision in an ageing population. However, as we have seen, under present policies of state pension provision (see the GAD calculations referred to above), there is no great pension crisis facing the UK. Rather, under existing policies, it seems that the continuing disparities between better-off and worse-off pensioners are likely to continue among future generations of retired people. Patchy work histories and family responsibilities will remain a cause of poverty in old age and paying for long-term care will be a growing problem, but state support for the better off is likely to become harder to justify. The challenge for the future is exemplified by the various types of minimum pension guarantees that have been proposed: to ensure some minimum standard of living in retirement, making best use of limited resources but avoiding the worst aspects of means-testing. There are no easy ways to meet this challenge but a little less attention on the looming 'crisis' seems justified and would give a little more room for manoeuvre.

▪ Summary

- Pensions, whether from the state, the employer or personal, are the main source of income in later life. Under present arrangements, levels of pensions payable on retirement depend directly on lifetime patterns of work and earnings. The patterns of work experienced by the baby boomers differ from those of previous generations in a number of ways that could be detrimental to their incomes in retirement:

- men's working lives are getting shorter as a consequence of later school-leaving and earlier retirement;
- job durations are declining;
- the proportion of baby boomers who had experienced unemployment by the age of 35 was very much higher than for any previous generation;
- baby boomers were more likely than any previous generation to have experienced self-employment by the age of 35;

but

- more women are in paid work, and it is likely that baby boomer women will have acquired more years of employment than the older generation.

- There has been an increase in membership of occupational pension schemes among women. Fewer second baby boom men are members of occupational pensions schemes than were previous generations. But both second baby boom men and women are more likely to have personal pensions.

- Between three-quarters and four-fifths of the first baby boomers will enter retirement owning their own homes. But more are expected to still have a mortgage than have today's older people.

- Compared with their counterparts in 1989/90, considerably greater proportions of the baby boomers will inherit house (or flat) property by the time they enter retirement.

- Complacency about the incomes in retirement of the baby boomers is premature – some of them will be better off than previous generations, but there will be continuing disparities between those who experienced full work histories and acquired pension rights and housing wealth and those who did not.

- The challenge for the future is to ensure some minimum standard of living in retirement, making the best use of limited resources but avoiding the worst aspects of means-testing.

▪ Acknowledgements

Material from the Family Expenditure Survey (FES), made available by the Office for National Statistics through the Data Archive, is Crown copyright and has been used with permission. Analyses of FES data have been conducted through the Gerontology Data Service at the Age Concern Institute of Gerontology. The author alone is responsible for the analysis and interpretation of data presented here. Thanks also go to Maria Evandrou and Jane Falkingham for comments on an earlier version of this chapter.

4 Health and health care

Gillian Dalley

Over the past thirty years the UK health care system has been transformed by a series of organisational and technological developments. During the same period, growing disparities have emerged in health status, wealth and employment opportunities. Changes in the structure of the labour market, highlighted in Chapter 2, are altering traditional expectations of stable careers and lifelong work. The complex relationship between all these changes has been the subject of considerable debate, and its impact on the experience of the baby boomers as they move towards retirement is as yet unknown. In trying to make an assessment of the prospects for health and the provision of health care into the next century, some overall judgement must be made about the interplay of current patterns and their consequences for the future.

In general, the period since the end of World War 2 has been marked by steady improvements in the nation's health. Mortality rates have fallen and life expectancy has continued to rise (see Chapter 1, Table 1.1). Infant mortality, in particular, has fallen dramatically. Such improvements, however, fit a continuous trend linked to changes in environment and behaviour over the last 100 years at least. Improvements in hygiene and nutrition, the introduction of public health measures and changes in reproductive behaviour (the age at which women are having children, the number of children, contraception, etc) have all played their part. The extent of the direct contribution of doctors and other health professionals within the formal health care system has to be considered alongside these broader influences (McKeown, 1979). Irrespective of the reasons for these general improvements, however, the baby boomers have been fortunate to benefit from their impact. Having experienced improved conditions in their youth and middle age, it might be assumed that they will go on to 'age well' or 'age healthily'.

There is another side to this, however. Although the picture looks relatively rosy at a general level, closer investigation raises doubts. The government's health strategy *The Health of the Nation*, published as a White Paper in 1992 (Secretary of State for Health, 1992), which sets out targets for improving the nation's health over the current decade and beyond, points to some disturbing trends. Cross-national comparisons demonstrate, for example, that the UK tops the league, after Ireland, for early deaths in men from circulatory diseases. In addition, life expectancy for both men and women is shown to be less in the UK than, for example, Japan, Greece and the Netherlands (Department of Health, 1993a). Furthermore, it appears that improvements in reducing death rates from all causes for men in the age group 15–44 seem to have tailed off in recent years. This, it appears, is due to the increased deaths from suicide, alcohol or drug abuse and AIDS. The second baby boom cohort (born 1961–65) have been particularly affected by the last, reaching sexual maturity around the time the virus was discovered but before the 'safe sex' campaigns. Testicular cancer is the most common new cancer experienced by men in the 25–34 age group. In the case of women's health, the death rate for lung cancer has risen steadily since 1970 and that for breast cancer remains disturbingly high. At present, these diseases are generally the ones that cause the greatest numbers of preventable deaths in people below 65 and are, consequently, those that apply most directly to the baby boomers. If they are to benefit from further improvements, it is imperative that the health strategy succeeds.

There is another matter for concern. Within the broad picture there are wide variations between different population groups within the UK itself. Socio-demographic factors associated with geography, ethnicity and social class all seem to have a bearing on variations in health status. How far these associations will persist in the face of strategies for change remains to be seen, but clearly they pose a major challenge to those responsible for shaping health and other aspects of social policy.

■ Baby boomers today: health status

The first baby boom cohort grew up in the 1950s and 1960s at a time of relative affluence, after wartime and post-war austerity had come to an end, employment rates were high and poverty was assumed to be vanquished. Theirs was the first generation to benefit fully from universal free-at-the-point-of-use NHS health care provision. Infant mortality rates had dropped substantially, from 50 per 1000 in 1930 to under 8 per 1000 by 1992, and life expectancy at birth was rising, from 58.7 years (males) and 62.9 (females) in 1930 to 67.9 (males) and 73.8 (females) in 1961 (Devis, 1990).

Entering their fifth decade of life now, as a group the first baby boomers are experiencing lowered death rates for a variety of conditions: between 1970 and 1990 the death rate from stroke for those under 65 fell from 25 per 100,000 to below 15, and from coronary heart disease from over 80 per 100,000 to 58. The diseases that were prevalent in an earlier generation – tuberculosis and poliomyelitis and a range of other infectious diseases – had fallen to almost nothing in their childhood. But there are now contemporary hazards that confront them (accidents, suicides, HIV/AIDS, BSE, diseases associated with lifestyle – diet and smoking). In addition, the transformation in lifestyle in other ways at both individual and societal level since World War 2 may have health consequences for both baby boom cohorts of which we are so far unaware. The industrial production of food, pollution from motor vehicles, a general lack of exercise from school age onwards may all cause health problems that are yet to be fully understood. Death rates from lung cancer are a good example of how the lifestyle habits and experiences at one stage in the life course have consequences for health status much later in life: in men the death rate had peaked by 1970 but for women who, as a category, became smokers at a later period, the rate is still rising (Secretary of State for Health, 1992).

The experiences of the two baby boom generations can be followed by tracking them over the period from when they reached adulthood to their approaching middle age, using data from the General Household Survey (GHS) (Evandrou and Falkingham, 1997). Evidence on the health of the baby boomers using such data is mixed. One widely used indicator of health status is the existence of a long-standing illness and whether that illness limits a person's activity at all. Figures 4.1 and 4.2 present the proportion of men and women from three birth cohorts that report having a limiting long-standing illness at a particular age. Those born in 1946–50 can be thought of as representative of the first baby boom, whilst those born in 1961–65 represent the second baby boomers. The people born in 1931–35 are those who are approaching retirement or are recently retired today. As is expected, the proportion of each cohort reporting a limiting long-standing illness rises with age. Moreover, successive younger generations appear to report slightly *higher* levels of limiting long-standing illness than the previous generation at the same age, and women report slightly higher levels than men. At the age of 29, 11 per cent of women in the youngest cohort report having a limiting long-standing illness, compared with 8 per cent of women in the 1946–50 cohort at the same age. This may reflect a general rise in the propensity to report ill-health, regardless of age or generation. Alternatively, it may reflect *real* differences in health status between the generations, with younger generations reporting progressively worse health at the same stage in the life course. However, it may also represent larger numbers of people

Figure 4.1 Proportion of women reporting limiting long-standing illness, by birth cohort (3-year moving averages)

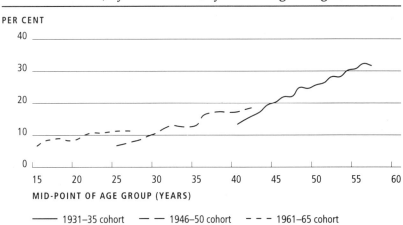

Source: Evandrou and Falkingham (1997, Figure 13).

living successfully with a chronic condition, who might previously have died in childhood.

The Carnegie Inquiry Report, *Health: Abilities and wellbeing*, suggested that smoking is the single largest factor accounting for the ill-health of older people today. If we look at the proportion who currently smoke (Figures 4.3 and 4.4), fewer people from each successive cohort report that they smoke at a given age. And the trend to give up smoking is clear within each cohort. It is interesting that men appear to be 'giving up' at a greater rate than women. By the age of 40, a greater proportion of first baby boomer women smoke than men. Given that smoking is known to be related to a wide variety of ill-nesses and health states, evidence of decreased prevalence may suggest that tomorrow's older people may be healthier than today's.

Another influence on health is the level of stress faced within the workplace. Britain's workers work the longest hours in Europe (CSO, 1996). Moreover, 30 per cent of British workers reported that they found their work stressful and 44 per cent reported that they 'often or always' came home from work 'exhausted' (Curtice, 1993). Evandrou and Falkingham (1997), again using GHS data, found that the second baby boomer men have experienced longer working weeks at earlier

Figure 4.2 Proportion of men reporting limiting long-standing illness, by birth cohort (3-year moving averages)

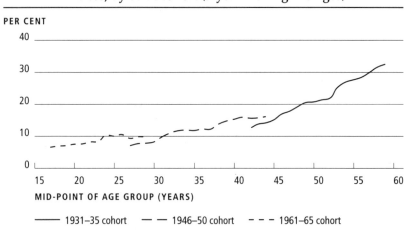

Source: Evandrou and Falkingham (1997, Figure 13).

stages in their life course than the preceding generations. By 30 years of age, 20 per cent of men in the 1961–65 cohort in employment reported working 50 or more hours per week, compared with 13 per cent of men in the 1946–50 cohort at the same age. Longer hours worked at younger ages may adversely affect health (directly or indirectly) both now and in later life.

It is difficult to generalise about the health of each cohort but if we look *within* the cohorts, as previous chapters have indicated, there are striking disparities in their experiences to date. The 1980s were beneficial to one section of the second baby boomers in particular – that group commonly referred to as 'yuppies' – they had good jobs, high salaries and great opportunities. For many of them this may still be the case and will continue to be so. But for some, when the economic boom was over, so were their prospects. At the same time there has been another group within the cohort who have seen few of the benefits of the 1980s. They have experienced continuing unemployment, which is often likely to have been geographically determined as the

Figure 4.3 Proportion of women currently smoking, by birth cohort

Source: Evandrou and Falkingham (1997, Figure 17).

old industries closed down (coal and steel, for example) or because they were from an ethnic minority or lived in rundown areas of the inner cities. The consequences of these experiences for their present health status and as they move into retirement may well be significant.

We know from data published recently (Benzeval, Judge and Whitehead, 1995; Joseph Rowntree Foundation, 1995) that there has been a growing divide between rich and poor, which is bound to manifest itself in health terms over the coming years. People in unskilled occupations and their children are twice as likely to die prematurely than are those from professional groups, in infancy, in childhood and between the ages of 15 and 64. The steepest gradient is seen in deaths from accidents and from infectious and respiratory diseases. In addition, people from disadvantaged groups show more registrations for conditions such as cancers of the cervix, stomach and lung. The longitudinal Whitehall study of civil servants has shown clearly that men in the lowest occupational grades were three times more likely to die prematurely than those in the highest (Marmot et al, 1984), and this

Figure 4.4 Proportion of men currently smoking, by birth cohort

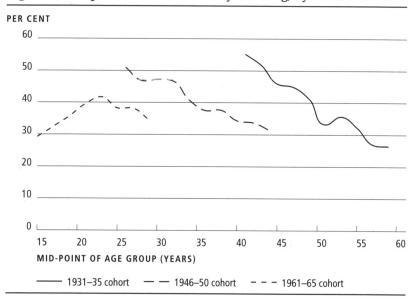

Source: Evandrou and Falkingham (1997, Figure 18).

persists throughout old age (Marmot and Shipley, 1996). Smaje (1995), reviewing the health status of minority ethnic groups, suggests that, although evidence is sparse, what there is shows increased ill-health and deaths with a possible association with the experience of unemployment rates that are twice as high as in the 'white' population.

■ Baby boomers in 2020: health trends

Predicting the health status of the baby boomers in 2020 depends on a number of assumptions. Some will be directly health-related, but others will be concerned with wider issues that have both a direct and an indirect impact on health. If we can assume that the targets set out in the *Health of the Nation* have been met (which relate to five broad areas of priority: coronary heart disease and stroke; cancers; mental illness; HIV/AIDS and sexual health; and accidents) the people reaching retirement age will have suffered fewer deaths from coronary heart disease, strokes and cancers and fewer will have died in accidents or as a result of suicide. A greater proportion will therefore be reaching retirement age, and in a healthier mental state, than have preceding generations. However, their experiences through life may have varied considerably one from another, in terms of both health and other life events.

As well as speculating on how current trends will develop for the baby boomers, further insight about the future may be gained by looking at the health status of older people today. At present, what evidence there is seems to suggest that health status converges between classes, the older people get. This is likely to be caused by the 'healthy survivor' effect, whereby those of all classes who survive into older age are the fittest of their respective generations. Differences are not wiped out, however, as is demonstrated by recent evidence from the Whitehall study (Marmot and Shipley, 1996) but less attention has been given by researchers generally to class differences in old age than to differences manifested before the age of 65 (Victor, 1994). This is due in part to problems of social classification after retirement but also to a concentration on premature deaths (defined as deaths before the age of 65) as being the measurable indicator for class inequalities in health. Nevertheless, experiences undergone before the age of 65 are likely to carry with them consequences into older age and affect different groups of people differentially. Victor has shown clear evidence for class- and gender-based differences in ill-health and deaths for men and women over 65. She found age-related increases in ill-health and death rates but, in general, older people from professional groups fared better than their counterparts in social classes IV and V.

Looking ahead into the twenty-first century, there are a number of factors to take into account. If, for example, we undergo another series of economic recessions between now and 2020 as we experienced in the 1980s and early 1990s, this will be bound to have an impact on the health of those most affected. The 1980s saw vigorous debate about the relationship between unemployment and health (Carr-Hill, 1987; Benzeval, Judge and Whitehead, 1995) but it is now generally accepted that there is a strong link between unemployment, poverty and ill-health. Significantly from this perspective, the proportion of those who remain economically inactive has grown over the years. Even now, with unemployment rates officially declining, the proportion of men in the 55–64 age group who are not economically active has been growing substantially, from under 9.7 per cent in 1970 to 31.6 per cent in 1988 (Walker et al, 1991). If this trend continues, as the first baby boomers and then the second grow older, a sizeable proportion of the men will experience non-employment (unemployment, invalidity, early retirement) with the negative impact for health that this implies. In contrast, fellow cohort members who remain in work will no doubt benefit from higher wages, the prospect of occupational pensions and the consequential benefits these may have for health. The experience of women is likely to be somewhat different. The numbers of women in the labour force have risen and will continue to do so, and so women retiring in 2020 will have had a record of working years behind them, although many will have worked part-time and many will not have contributed to occupational pension schemes.

In addition, the lifestyle effects of diet, smoking and the extent to which people take exercise and are subject to stress will also have long-term effects. It has long been a matter for dispute as to how effective health education messages are. One of the arguments in the debate about inequalities in health has been about how far seemingly 'lifestyle' activities that are harmful to health are amenable to individual control and how far they are structurally conditioned (Carr-Hill, 1987). If the latter theory is true, health education messages are doomed to failure and the deleterious consequences of certain social activities will continue to be felt by the baby boomers as they grow older. Blaxter (1990) has shown that the readiness of people to do things 'to keep healthy' varies by age, gender and class. Furthermore, at a policy level, insufficient research has been conducted and resources invested in measures to reduce the interrelated risk factors associated with premature death and preventable ill-health that threaten active life expectancy (Manton, 1989).

Moreover, once the baby boomers have reached retirement and move on into old age, what quality of life in terms of health experiences will they encounter? It is likely that the trend to longer life expectancy will continue, with the proportion of people over 75 increasing steadily in the first half of the next century. Currently, the diseases of old age develop substantially as people reach the eighth and ninth decades of life. Overwhelmingly, the degenerative diseases such as arthritis and rheumatism along with other bone and joint conditions prevail, followed by those relating to eyesight (cataract) and heart conditions (Department of Health, Central Health Monitoring Unit, 1992).

There are contrasting arguments about what the health status of older people is likely to be in 2020. On the one hand, if we extrapolate from today's evidence, it seems that the baby boomers in retirement will, like today's retired generation, develop heart and other circulatory diseases, certain cancers and a variety of degenerative conditions. If, however, the lessons of health education about improved diet, increased exercise, non-smoking and so on have been learnt (Manton, 1989; Walker and Walker 1993), it is suggested that people reaching retirement age in 2020 will be able to look forward to an increase in disability-free years of life as well as a longer life in total than their parents a generation earlier (Manton, 1986). There are disputes within the research community as to whether recent increases in life expectancy have been accompanied by an associated absence of disability – the 'compression of morbidity [ill-health]' hypothesis (Fries, 1983) – which will continue, or whether living longer beyond 75 is accompanied by increasing disability (Smith and Jacobson, 1988). On the positive side, there seems to be a trend in the UK to increased reporting of long-standing illness being less in people over 75, and in the USA increased life expectancy is beginning to be associated with a decline in age-specific disability (Tallis, 1994).

Nevertheless, as highlighted in the preceding chapters, it is important to point out that the cohort is heterogeneous. Those of higher social class, living in certain parts of the country, who retire after a lifetime of fulfilling work, with occupational pensions and a record of good health, are likely to experience a healthier old age than those of lower social class living in the north, Scotland or in the inner cities, with poor employment records, who have suffered from ill-health (sometimes related to occupation), who come from minority ethnic groups or who are poor.

There is another dimension to these comparisons. As people grow older, they often require increasing social support to help them in the conduct of their daily lives. The social policies of future governments will have an important bearing on how available this will be. Medical developments will clearly be important, but equally so will be what the state decides is its role in funding health and social care, housing and pensions. The most vulnerable people in relation to health status are also going to be the ones most affected by decisions taken in all these areas. Age discrimination already seems to be operating in relation to a variety of treatments and care (Thane, 1989; Whitaker, 1992; Seymour, 1993) and this may continue to grow.

▪ The health care system

The baby boomers will not be growing old in an organisational and administrative vacuum. The degree to which their health and social care needs are provided for by the state or on a private basis will depend largely on future political decisions about the NHS and the appropriate role of the state.

Since its inception in 1948, the NHS has been both praised and criticised. There is no doubt that during the first thirty years there was a general consensus that the benefits derived by individuals were considerable. The impact on people at large of the availability of health care that was free at the point of use cannot be overstated. In terms of access (free) and availability (the expansion of the family doctor and community health services as well as hospital services), the population benefited greatly. How far improvements in the general health of the population are directly attributable to the NHS and how far they are related to other socio-economic factors operating at the same time, however, is a matter for debate. Nevertheless, public attitudes are almost wholly positive in their views about the benefits conferred by the health service.

By the 1970s, debate began about the future direction of the health service, with the establishment of the Royal Commission on the future of the NHS. This, however, was overtaken during the following decade with the advent of the Thatcher government pledged to radicalising most social and economic institutions in the country; the NHS was no exception. Profound structural changes were proposed, being put into effect in 1990 with the NHS and Community Care Act. One of the intentions of these changes – notably the introduction of the division between purchasing and providing services – was to make the costs of treatments far more explicit. Inevitably, one of the consequences of this in the context of resource constraint was to raise the issues of rationing and of excluding certain forms of care and treatment from NHS responsibility (McKee and Laing, 1993). There has also been a growing debate about how far changes in the demographic profile of society, with the increase in the numbers of the very old (that is, 85-plus), will constitute a 'burden' on society and therefore precipitate fundamental changes in the way health and social care are funded (Thane, 1989).

In these changing circumstances, what does the future hold for the baby boomers? What will they be able to expect of the health care system in 2020? Will the hopes and expectations that characterised their parents' outlook hold good for them too?

Characteristics of the health care system today

The health service is at a point of transition. This is due in part to the changes brought about by political dogma – the development of the internal market in which one hospital or community trust is expected to compete with another for 'business', along with the opening up of the state system to private finance and the purchasing of care within the private sector by NHS health authorities. But there are other changes rooted in changing attitudes to care needs on the one hand and technological developments on the other. Styles of nursing care have undergone profound changes over the past forty years. Patients no longer stay in bed for long periods after operations. The expectation now is that people go into hospital for short periods of time and are discharged within a few days, or even on the same day of treatment. There is a widespread view that people prefer to stay at home if at all possible, particularly in the case of chronic illness or infirmity. The development of community care has been predicated on this perspective. In addition, developments in medical technology, anaesthetics and drug therapies have made it possible for treatments to be provided much less invasively than before (through techniques such as 'keyhole' surgery), with consequences for the length of time taken for recovery.

These changes have led to two major changes in the pattern of health care provision. First there has been the development of community care policy. People who in earlier times would have been cared for in long-stay institutions are now expected to be cared for 'in the community' – most often at home, supported by an array of community health and social care services and by members of their families or friends and neighbours. Different arguments have been put forward to explain the ascendancy of the policy of community care, ranging from the ideological to the economic (Dalley, 1996). Second, there has been much talk of the transition from secondary to primary care. This relates to the recent developments in the health care system's ability to treat people outside hospitals because of improved and developing technologies. The primary care services (general practitioners (GPs) and the primary health care team) are now increasingly being expected to take on responsibility for treatments such as minor surgery that were previously provided in hospital. This has major implications for the organisation and funding of primary care, and for the professionals expected to provide it. Although there has been a shift in funding towards the family health services (primary care) over the past 25 years from 31 per cent of the health budget to 45 per cent (Chew, 1995), there will have to be an even greater growth of the sector to meet current policy expectations.

There have been other significant developments within primary care under the reforms introduced at the start of the 1990s. In addition to GPs being encouraged to provide a wider range of treatments in the surgery, they have also been encouraged to become fundholders – that is, to be responsible for purchasing care from secondary providers (hospitals). Individual practices hold the budget for purchasing care for their patients and thus act as a separate purchasing arm distinct from district health authorities that hold a broad responsibility for purchasing care for the whole population in their catchment area.

In the early days of the scheme, fundholders were limited to purchasing a small range of treatments but the scheme is gradually being extended both in terms of the numbers of GPs involved and in the range of treatments they can purchase. Currently there are a number of pilot practices that are purchasing the whole range of treatment and care available (NHS Executive, 1995). This trend, if it persists, will have a dramatic impact on the future of strategic planning in the health service. If purchasing is in the hands of a substantial number of uncoordinated general practices, each purchasing on behalf of its patients, the role of district health authorities in being able to think ahead and to commission and purchase on the basis of wider population need will be curtailed. Furthermore, with individual GPs having to make clinical decisions about individual patients, which have a clear financial tag on each one, questions must arise as to how those decisions will be reached. Issues of equity, subjectivity, priority and fairness in decision-making will all be played out in the privacy of the consulting room. The need for transparency and accountability is clear but so far little concern has been expressed about these issues.

Other trends within primary care relate to the respective roles of the professionals involved in delivering the service (NHS Management Executive, 1993). Nurses are seeking to expand their role, establishing new responsibilities as nurse practitioners at the interface between doctors and their traditional nursing role. A number of pilot schemes have placed nurse practitioners in novel settings, such as in pharmacies, accident and emergency departments, and day centres for homeless people, with the aim of giving increased clinical responsibility to the nurse and making primary care more accessible to a wide range of people (Touche Ross, 1994). These initiatives have been in line with the thinking contained in the Tomlinson report (1992) on the future of health care in London, which stressed the need to shift the balance from secondary to primary care settings.

Impact on the baby boomers

It is hard to judge what the future of the NHS will be. Changes in direction are likely to be guided by political decision as much as by further developments driven by technology and scientific knowledge within the health system itself. Continuation of recent policies would mean that the impetus towards breaking up the system and introducing more market-driven changes would be maintained. It is likely that there would be three sorts of development:

- Further fragmentation of the national structure of the service (building on the introduction of Trusts and GP fundholding) so that planning decisions are made locally and geographical disparities develop in what services are available.

- Further privatisation of the system with the introduction of private finance to develop NHS services themselves and increasing purchase of private sector services on the part of NHS purchasing authorities (health authorities and GP fundholders), NHS providers increasingly selling services to private patients.

- The withdrawal of the NHS from responsibility to provide certain services and an expectation that individuals meet the costs of these services themselves through private insurance schemes, in spite of the likelihood that this will prove too expensive for individuals.

The implications for the baby boomers are significant. Geographical disparities already exist and to have them increase will mean that people entering middle and older age (ie those who are typically high users of the service) will be particularly affected. With greater concentrations of private sector services, and an abandonment of the principle of universal provision, poorer sections of society (very often older people) will lose out. The services most likely to be dropped by the NHS are those that are already being affected – that is, long-term care for older people. In addition, rationing of NHS treatments by age may also develop more explicitly in the bid to keep NHS expenditure down. As the need to take out insurance for long-term care and other treatments develops, the cost characteristics of insurance-based systems may come into play (Culyer, 1991). Instead of being a lean and low-cost service, the health system in the UK will become more expensive – at a cost to individuals themselves.

A major cause for concern in respect of these possibilities is the gradual and unpredictable nature of their introduction. If private, insurance-based provision is to be the preferred outcome, government needs to plan decades in advance to allow people to prepare for the change. However, the experience of today's older people has been that withdrawal from providing long-term care has taken place rapidly and unannounced; if that pattern is repeated, the baby boomers will be in great difficulties. Even if due notice were given, it might not be effective, and would certainly be unpopular. The reception that greeted the government discussion document *A New Partnership in Care* (Chancellor of the Exchequer and Secretaries of State, 1996), which suggested partial private insurance to offset the costs of long-term care, suggests that such moves would be unacceptable to many older people.

Private provision based on individuals planning ahead depends on those individuals having the ability to enter into long-term pension and insurance arrangements. As Chapter 3 discusses, even today the number of people contributing to private (both personal and occupational) pensions is insufficient to ensure a pensioner population in the future that will be generally self-sufficient. According to a report by the Social Security Advisory Committee (1994), only 47 per cent of current employees are members of occupational pension schemes, 28 per cent of male employees and 19 per cent of female employees having personal pension plans. Many of the plans proposed for the future are predicated on an assumption that this proportion will increase substantially. However, as Chapter 2 shows, patterns of working are undergoing profound changes with fewer individuals entering into stable occupations that have employer pensions attached. Policies constructed on an assumption that most working people will be able to provide their own pensions and health care insurance are likely to fail if these patterns persist (Hutton, 1995). Furthermore, the current trends of early work exit (much of it far from voluntary) will have be reversed to ensure longer participation in the labour force to the benefit of both individuals and society as a whole (Henretta, 1994; Gregg and Wadsworth, 1995).

If, however, the political mood changes, future developments in the health system are hard to predict. First, it is not clear whether an alternative government would seek to undo recent decisions completely or if it would simply modify present arrangements. It is probable that an attempt would be made to introduce a national strategy for the health service, setting out priorities and intentions for application nation-wide, thus reversing some of the effects of current fragmentation. However, it may be that such a national planning system would confirm current trends: a decision might be made that present moves to withdraw from the provision of long-term care, for example, would be confirmed and that charges for domiciliary care could be imposed. There is little indication (at the time of writing) among the opposition parties that a decision to uphold the principle of NHS provision of long-term care, free at the point of use, is going to be made – irrespective of what the majority of people might wish. Radical ideas are sometimes floated, such as a hypothecated tax designed exclusively to fund healthcare expenditure (Davies and Chandler, 1994), but the likelihood of their being adopted seems remote.

In relation to some of the other developments in health care, present trends are likely to continue, whatever government is in power. The current emphasis on community-based care and attempts to shift the balance from the secondary to the primary care sector will persist. This ought to mean that, as the baby boomers get older and require medical treatment, they are more than ever likely to receive some of that treatment in the doctor's surgery or at home. General practices are likely to become more accessible and better equipped both in the facilities they offer and in the staff based there. Whether GPs continue to develop their practices as businesses under the fundholding scheme or moves are made, as tentatively anticipated in the *Making London Better* proposals (limited in the case of that document to difficult areas of the inner city), to develop a salaried GP service in which GPs are salaried staff members of the NHS (Department of Health, 1993b) – and outlined more clearly in the White Paper on primary care (Department of Health, Welsh Office and Scottish Office, 1996) – will depend on political decisions. Similarly, the degree to which GPs employ other professional staff directly or whether primary health care teams develop on a more collegial basis, as groups of colleagues in partnership, will depend on wider political decisions about the primacy of GPs as employers and leaders of staff in the team.

What is certain is that, if more care and treatment do take place locally in the surgery or at home, it will be essential for doctors, nurses and paramedical staff to be trained to deliver it effectively (Tomlinson, 1992). The need for continuing post-qualifying education will grow as more and more sophisticated techniques become available. Professionals trained in one decade will no longer be skilled to cope with the advances achieved in another, if updating and refresher training are not available. The overseeing of these major training and human resource issues may be compromised if the fragmentation of the service proceeds; a *national* health service does at least guarantee some strategic overview of the complex interrelationship between the varied components of the service.

With care increasingly being delivered in the home – this relates both to the long-term care of dependent (usually older) people and to acute treatment through 'hospital at home' schemes and GP treatment – attention will have to be given to people's capacity to be cared for at home. On whom will the responsibility lie? Underlying much of the thinking in the health care system is an assumption that there will be relatives or neighbours 'back in the community' to support individuals requiring care. In 1989, 36 per cent of people over the age of 65 lived alone (Department of Health, Central Health Monitoring Unit, 1992). Jane Falkingham, in Chapter 1, showed that this proportion is likely to have increased by the time the baby boomers reach retirement age. Furthermore, it appears that more of the second baby boomers are deciding not to have children (see Chapter 1, Figures 1.7

and 1.8). If these predictions turn out to be accurate, many of the baby boomers will enter old age with no immediate family to support them.

■ Conclusion

The baby boomers face a perplexing future. On the one hand, trends look good. More preventable deaths will be avoided, in line with the government's health strategy, although this will benefit some sections within the cohort more than others. Life expectancy will increase, along with the likelihood that the extra years gained may well be free from disability. The aim of dying young at an old age (Smith and Jacobson, 1988) will be the norm for an increasing number of people. At the same time, health care will be accessible, local and community based. Fewer resources will be locked into expensive acute hospitals to the detriment of the primary care services. This is the optimistic forecast.

On the other hand, there is another possibility: with more people living longer, and with society failing to fulfil its part of the contract to sustain and support all its citizens, there is a danger for those among the old who are sick that they become a social group discriminated against and vulnerable. In addition, there may be consequences of the conditions of modern living that have yet to make themselves apparent. The recent growth in the prevalence of asthma is explained by some as being caused by air pollution, particularly in cities, created by the combustion engine. The use of pesticides, advances in food technology and genetic engineering in animal farming, for example, may all have consequences for health of which we are as yet unaware and which may manifest themselves in later life.

Furthermore, the gloomy predictions made currently by the opponents of the health reforms and by those seeking to retain the major hospitals threatened with closure may turn out to be correct. They argue that the internal market simply means a proliferation of managers and accountants and that there has been a gross underestimate of the needs of those in the big conurbations for acute hospital care. If this is so, the poor, the sick and the vulnerable (among whom will be found some of the baby boomers) are those likely to suffer the consequences most severely as costs rise, rationing becomes established and the state withdraws increasingly from its traditional responsibility to care for all citizens. This is the worst outcome. Which forecast will prevail, however, so far remains unclear.

■ Summary

- ■ Evidence on the future health of the baby boomers is mixed:
  - – trends in smoking provide one indication that the baby boomers may be healthier in later life than today's older people;
  - – however, the proportion who report limiting long-standing illness suggests the opposite;
  - – higher unemployment and longer working weeks for those in work may also result in poorer health later on.

- ■ In reality, health status is complex and cannot easily be represented by a single indicator. Forecasting health status trends is yet more difficult and uncertain, and it is not clear what the health of tomorrow's older people will be.

- ■ As with income, there will be wide variations in health status *within* the baby boom cohorts.

- ■ Trends towards further privatisation of the health system will exacerbate inequalities among the baby boomers.

- ■ Those with uneven employment histories may not be in a position to contribute either to private pensions or to private health insurance. Yet, given that employment and occupation are related to health, these groups may be the most in need of that health care.

5 Community care

Jane Lewis

It is probably easier to predict the needs of the baby boomers in respect of community care in 2020 than it is to predict the nature of social care provision. It is unlikely that ten years ago anyone would have accurately foreseen the change that has taken place since 1988 in the provision of all social services, including health, education and housing, as well as community care. The introduction of market principles into these services, together with a shift in ideas as to whom they are meant to serve, is in the process of substantially changing the expectations of the late-middle aged as to what they may 'count on' in their old age. Although it is possible that we may achieve supportive communities of some kind early in the next century, this chapter assumes that the current changes will not easily or quickly be reversed and seeks to explore their implications.

As ever, future needs will probably be graduated, from help with shopping, gardening and housework, to help with intimate personal care, to constant nursing attention. It is likely that the first baby boomers, who will probably be the only people to have grown up assuming that state welfare provision would be available, would prefer the security of knowing that the full range of their needs will be catered for, and they will certainly expect the quality of care to be high.

The provision of social care has always been mixed; since World War 2, it has always involved the family, the voluntary sector, the private sector and the state, albeit that the balance between these has changed significantly over time. The problem in predicting the future lies in forecasting how much and what kind of 'free' care – state or informal – will be available to baby boomers. Maria Evandrou, in

Chapter 6, evaluates the latter, whilst here I concentrate on the former, although the two are far from being mutually exclusive.

▪ What might be expected of future community care policies?

Community care has always been something of a 'motherhood' issue in the thinking of both political left and right. Richard Titmuss wrote of the way in which it conjured up 'a sense of warmth and human kindness, essentially personal and comforting, as loving as the wild flowers so enchantingly described by Lawrence in *Lady Chatterly's Lover*' (Titmuss, 1968). However, the meaning of 'community care' has always been vague. Alan Walker (1982) suggested that the term's 'durability probably owes much to its manipulation to encompass the widest possible range of institutions', whereas Roy Parker has concluded that its meaning

> has been changed to suit the new policies; its catchphrase character has obscured the complexities of care; it has invested a hotchpotch of policies and practices with a spurious sense of integration and consistency and because of its attractive connotations it has tended to escape close critical scrutiny. (Sinclair et al, 1990)

What these comments indicate is the extent to which community care has tended to mean all things to all people. For example, to staff in the NHS, all residential care that is not hospital care counts as community care, whereas this is unlikely to be so for either staff in social services departments or their clients. The comments also hint at the extent to which community care polices have been something of a 'poor relation', rarely at the top of the political agenda for their own sake. This has been the position for almost fifty years and has indeed characterised the most recent community care reforms. It would be overly optimistic to expect a dramatic change in the priorities of policy makers over the next twenty-five years, although it is possible that the first and second waves of baby boomers may contribute to an intensified ageing lobby along the lines of the disability lobby in recent years. On the other hand, policy could swing further to the political right and towards the market.

A survey of recent policy change provides some hints as to how policy might develop in the future. The 1990 NHS and Community Care Act appeared to attach considerable weight to community care, at least in so far as it was concerned with the welfare of older people. However, it was issues to do with the social security budget and with the NHS that drove the community care provisions. When the Act gave local authorities new responsibilities for community care, it arguably gave them responsibility for what was likely to prove a major mopping-up operation. In 1990 Government was responding above all to the explosion in the Department of Social Security's expenditure for residential care during the 1980s, which had been caused by the open-ended subsidy given to it by the reform of social security in the early 1980s. There was a 57 per cent increase in residential care provision for older people between 1980 and 1991 (Wistow et al, 1994). Given that residential care was the only way people had of spending social security funds, it is not clear how many would have chosen this form of provision rather than domiciliary services had they been an option. Certainly, there has been considerable disagreement as to how many people entering residential care in the 1980s 'needed' to do so (Audit Commission, 1986; Bradshaw and Gibbs, 1988; Committee of Public Accounts, 1988; Sinclair et al, 1990).

The only way of curbing the increase in Department of Social Security spending was to make local authorities the rationing agents. The only way to make this politically acceptable was to emphasise that the transfer of money would not swell local authority bureaucracy and to reassure the private sector by using the language of 'enabling' and promising that local authorities would become the purchasers of social care rather than direct providers. Authorities were required to spend the vast majority of the money transferred from the social security budget in the independent sector, and the 1997 White Paper, *A New Partnership for Care in Old Age* (Secretary of State for Social Security, 1997) on social services proposes to end all direct provision by local authorities.

In addition, changes within the NHS were also influential in pushing community care reform. Between 1982 and 1994, the number of acute hospital beds fell by almost a quarter; average length of stay fell by more than a third; throughput increased by over 80 per cent; and day case admissions grew by more than 200 per cent. Older people accounted for the use of 47 per cent of all acute bed days (days in hospitals) in 1992/3 and also for the fastest growth rate since 1989 in numbers of 'finished consultant episodes' (completed referrals to a hospital specialist) (Wistow, 1995). The reorganisation of the acute hospital in line with technological advances such as 'keyhole' and 'day' surgery has led to a desire on the part of the NHS to reduce its provision of continuing care. How far down this particular line the NHS will be able to go is not clear, but the Secretary of State, Mrs Virginia Bottomley, stated her view (in June 1994) that the idea of spending a night in hospital would become 'a curiosity'.

Thus in the early 1990s community care was developed in relation to the problems of the social security budget and the NHS; service delivery by itself was not at the forefront of government thinking. Rather, it was the rationale for the new policy that emphasised issues of service delivery. Thus the Policy Guidance stressed that the separation of purchasing from providing within social services departments, such that local authorities became 'enablers', would weaken the influence of providers' vested interests in the identification of needs and services, and would introduce competition into the supply of service, thereby increasing choice and responsiveness to need. The Guidance held out the promise of moving from service-led care, whereby clients' needs were fitted into existing services, to needs-led care, whereby services would be tailored to clients and enable them to live as independent lives as possible 'in the community' (Department of Health, 1990).

However, the main factor driving policy was resources, and it is not surprising that there was conflict within the community care reforms between moving to needs-led services and resourcing those services. The 1990 Act made it clear that it was to be the local authority that defined need, not the user of the service. Choice was to reside in range of supply, not in the direct exercise of preference by the consumers of care. The 1990 Policy Guidance advised:

> local authorities also have a responsibility to meet needs within the resources available and this will sometimes involve difficult decisions where it will be necessary to strike a balance between meeting the needs

identified within available resources and meeting the care preferences of the individual. (Department of Health, 1990)

Thus clients are no nearer to being sure that their preferences will be met.

The tension between needs and resources is hardly new. John Baldock (1994) has suggested that, although the personal social services have experienced two periods of growth in resources, they have been 'supply determined'. Despite pretensions to universality following the formation of the Seebohm social services departments in the early 1970s, the personal social services have always been residual and staff in those departments have always been resource rationers. Baldock has also suggested that need has historically been a very small part of the business of the personal social services: 'In fact there are few reasons to expect that in the 1990s the supply of services will or can respond directly to changes in social need' (ibid, p 163). In fact, until the 1970s, the personal social services did very little for whole categories of clients, particularly older people (Means and Smith, 1985). As late as 1985, the Audit Commission revealed that 85 per cent of older people had no contact with social services departments.

It is unlikely that all needs will be met on a collective basis in the future as it has been in the past. The question is whether need is likely to outstrip supply still further in the future. It may be that it will. The baby boomers are by definition numerous and although their health may well remain good in young and middle old age, there is no reason to think that they will escape entirely the deterioration that we are already beginning to associate with the 'old old'. Certainly, as Table 1.3 illustrates, the proportion of ethnic minority elders will be greater and whereas it is all too often assumed that family care is stronger in ethnic minority communities, we know far too little about the likely needs of these groups. In addition, if changes in the health service do move along the lines suggested by Mrs Bottomley, then, as Gillian Dalley points out in Chapter 4, there will be many more heavily dependent people 'in the community' seeking help from social services, whether in residential or domiciliary care.

▪ What needs are likely to be met and by whom?

The new policy of community care, implemented in April 1993, insisted that the assessment of need be separated from the provision of service, because only in this way could the real needs of people approaching social services departments be established. Past practice, it was held, had tended to fit clients to existing services, rather than seeking out services from a range of suppliers that would actually meet need. However, given the basic conflict between needs and resources it has proved very difficult to separate them in this ideal fashion.

Richards (1994) has neatly summarised the problem from the point of view of the social services' staff member:

> Separating the assessment of needs from a subsequent decision about eligibility depends in fact on the concept of need being operationalised independently of the agency policy and guidelines that are to determine what is to count as need, and that is where the difficulty lies.

Juliet Cheetham (1993) similarly insisted that

> assessment must remain rooted in the appreciation of the realities of services provision', and that 'it is not sensible to separate rigidly "needs talk" from "service talk". The assessment of older people with complex needs is a continuing process, impossible to disentangle from negotiation and service provision.

It may seem pointless to a social worker to assess a client as being in need of 'help with food' rather than being in need of meals on wheels, if she knows that the latter is effectively all that is available. Even if a wide range of services is known to be available, individually tailored packages of care take a great deal of staff time to arrange, as well as raising problems of monitoring, and may also prove more expensive. Studies to date show how difficult it is for local authorities to be truly creative in 'care packaging' and how most purchasers have continued to use 'off-the-shelf' or 'set list' services (Baldock and Ungerson, 1994; Hoyes et al, 1994; Lewis and Glennerster, 1996). Similarly, although local authorities have invested relatively heavily in training staff to operate the new purchaser/provider split, training will continue to be a pressing need for the independent sector as well as local authority providers if flexible services are to be achieved, but money is likely to be tight.

Thus, although the aim of the new community care policy to make services more responsive to need was admirable, it comes up against the problem of resources in two ways:

- It will tend to be cheaper and easier to provide whatever 'bulk' services are available. It has, in fact, proved difficult for authorities to stimulate the independent market for social care. With domiciliary provision, it has often been necessary to inject a large amount of money to produce a response, which results in a block contract. Whilst this may succeed in providing more flexible care, for example more weekend and evening home care, it will not necessarily make it possible to provide individually tailored care.

- Social services departments have been criticised in the past for 'warehousing' clients (providing services and care 'in bulk'), often in large institutions. The desire to meet need in more appropriate ways long pre-dates the 1990 reforms. However, 'warehousing' was relatively cheap. One of the hopes of the 1990s reforms was that domiciliary care could be provided as cheaply as institutional care. This seemed to be the message from the pilot work of the Personal Social Services Research Unit (PSSRU) during the 1980s, which targeted people on the verge of residential care and showed that gains in their quality of life could be made at no greater cost by keeping them in the community (Davies et al, 1990). However, the PSSRU researchers stressed the importance of carefully targeting the clients for this kind of care. Since 1993, there has been remarkably little effort to monitor the cost of domiciliary care packages compared to institutional provision, and in many authorities the inadequacies of unit costings make it impossible to do so. However, some authorities are already imposing a ceiling on what they are prepared to spend on a domiciliary package. It is possible that in the future, when faced with much larger numbers of heavily dependent people, 'warehousing' might return to the agenda.

Baby boomers have been schooled first in the often paternalistic ways of the post-war welfare state, and more recently have been encouraged to act as knowledgeable consumers in the social care marketplace. The ideas of choice and of flexible, appropriate and responsive services tailored to need would doubtless appeal to many but it has not proved easy to implement the 1990 reforms in these respects. Given that we can expect the tension between needs and resources to continue and the numbers needing care to increase, the prospects for the future do not seem overly hopeful.

The conflict between needs and resources also means that ways have to be found of reconciling them. The PSSRU researchers pointed out that particular social services had historically been expected to achieve policy goals for quite different types of client. Home helps, for example, had traditionally been used to monitor those believed to be at risk and to encourage, motivate and act as confidantes, as well as to perform tasks for frail older people. Thus their services had been offered to a general population of older people not at risk, to people at high risk of institutional care, to people who had suffered a fall or other health accident or who needed short-term help, and to informal carers bearing large burdens (Davies et al, 1990). Between 1980 and 1985 there had been a slight increase in home care provision, but the service was spread more widely rather than targeting those most in need (Bebbington and Davies, 1993). This led the researchers to comment on the apparent lack of sophisticated targeting of services, on the lack of criteria for stopping service and on the lack of data as to outcomes for clients.

The PSSRU researchers emphasised the importance of screening clients properly in order to ensure effective targeting. However, local authorities dealing with people requesting assessment have found it necessary to establish firm eligibility criteria in order to set limits on who may receive services. Indeed, at the end of 1993, the Audit Commission warned authorities that such criteria should allow 'just enough people with needs to exactly use up their budget (or be prepared to adjust their budgets)' (Audit Commission, 1993).

Since the implementation of the community care reforms, social services departments have had to decide on criteria for prioritising need. Most have done so on the basis of professional judgement as to the existing degrees of risk, dependency and statutory responsibility. Ways of determining priorities have varied considerably. The District

Audit Service (1992) promoted the idea of needs-led budgeting, which required social services departments to define levels of need as low, medium and high; to estimate the numbers of users at each level; to define the care components for each level of need; and to agree and to cost standard levels of service. This amounts to a determination of priorities over all and has enabled authorities who use it to work out how many clients with complex needs they can afford to provide for. Clients have to be deemed highly dependent before they are eligible for a complex assessment and hence for service. Social isolation, for example, is no longer sufficient reason for providing residential care.

One local authority investigated by Lewis, Glennerster and Sainsbury (1996) had developed a 'risk/needs matrix', the vertical axis of which records the area of primary need, physical taking priority over social, while the horizontal axis records the risk the client has within the area of his or her primary need. The client is then allocated a score. This authority decided that it would devote 84 per cent of its expenditure to purchasing services on behalf of clients falling in the top categories of priority 1–3.

It is thus possible to see a definition of need emerging from the process of setting priorities and determining eligibility for service. Need is linked firmly to physical dependency and risk, and hence to resources available. Clients at the same level of deterioration may be accorded different priority on account of the willingness and ability of a carer to cope. Perhaps inevitably, 'need' is translating into those whom social services departments cannot ignore. This becomes more significant for the future if older people are not provided with appropriate rehabilitation and convalescent facilities, given that clients are likely to become more heavily dependent as continuing care under the NHS is run down and the number of old old increases. If dependency levels increase and eligibility criteria become more tightly drawn, some clients must surely 'fall off the end'. Clients who are not at high risk and whose needs are for services such as shopping or cleaning may be more and more likely not to have those needs met. Indeed the theory of 'needs-led services' promotes the setting of priorities that legitimise not meeting lower level needs. The long-term effects of the decision to concentrate on meeting the needs of highly dependent people are unknown, but must raise questions about 'prevention' in the sense of sustaining people at home, which can only become more urgent. As early as 1993, the House of Commons Health Committee first raised the possibility of less dependent people having to enter institutions if their relatively more simple, but nevertheless vital, needs for service are not met. The conclusion of Allen et al (1992) at the end of their study of the views of elderly people living at home and in institutional care is worth revisiting:

> It is possible that there has been too much concentration on intensive packages of care and that the real point of community care has been missed. Targeting those 'most in need' and providing services for them may, in fact, be easier than caring for those who are less obviously in need. The lessons from this research suggest that more preventative services for more people may perhaps be of greater overall value in keeping elderly people out of residential care than concentrating services on a very few.

The problem is that at present we do not know. By 2020 we probably shall.

When the Audit Commission urged local authorities to adopt clear eligibility criteria, it pointed out that authorities had only a limited number of ways to contain expenditure. If they did not set firm eligibility criteria, they could only refuse to provide services or charge for services. As became increasingly apparent during 1994 and 1995, unlike health care, social care need not necessarily be free of charge, even when it is provided by a local authority. The diminution, and possibly in the future the ending, of continuing care under the NHS means that more older people will have to pay for nursing home care. Many local authorities have also begun to increase their charges for domiciliary services, and a report issued by the Local Government Anti-Poverty Unit late in 1994 concluded that in authorities where this had happened the take-up of services had dropped noticeably (Association of Metropolitan Authorities, 1994). Both the Conservative Party and the Social Justice Commission set up by the Labour Party concluded in 1994 that people who had accumulated savings and equity in the form of a house or flat should be expected to pay towards their care in old age. Data presented by Ruth Hancock in Chapter 3 suggest that some of the first wave of baby boomers will be in a position to do this, but the prospects for the second wave are less clear. The removal of job security during the late 1980s and 1990s and the creation of a flexible labour force have posed a threat to financial security in later life.

For baby boomers who do not meet the eligibility criteria for collectively provided care and cannot pay for it themselves, what will there be? The most continuous form of community care historically has been that provided by the family. During the 1980s, central government stressed the importance of 'informal' care. The 1981 White Paper *Growing Older* set off the great battle of the prepositions: whether community care properly meant care in or by the community. During the mid-1980s, there was a burgeoning feminist literature on the burdens borne by informal carers (eg Finch and Groves, 1983; Ungerson, 1987; Lewis and Meredith, 1988) and increasingly effective pressure from groups such as the Carers National Association. The 1990 reforms aimed to be both user and carer centred, the emphasis being less on passing the burden to informal carers than on helping them to care. However, when resources are limited, it is unclear how much influence can be brought to bear by the carer who is just about coping. The 1995 Carers (Recognition and Services) Act gave carers the right to an independent assessment of their own needs, but no concomitant right to services.

All the evidence suggests that women in particular want to care and there is no reason to suppose that this will change. However, data presented by Jane Falkingham in Chapter 1 raises considerable doubt over the prospective pool of carers who might be available to the baby boomers, particularly those from the second wave. In the 1950s the most common carer was the unmarried daughter; by the 1980s it was a spouse or a married woman in middle middle age. As Maria Evandrou discusses in Chapter 6, the rapid changes in family make-up during the 1980s and 1990s – such as the increasing numbers of childless marriages, of extramarital births and of divorce – make future patterns of informal care uncertain. It could be that the growth in 'blended families', through more separation, divorce and remarriage, will effectively increase the pool of carers, or we might be heading for ever-more dissociated individualism.

▪ Conclusion

Many people are optimistic about the prospects for the baby boomers, anticipating improved health and increased leisure and material wealth. Some also feel that the first wave of baby boomers will do better in terms of providing mutual aid. In other words, some more informal forms of voluntary help will come into being, substituting for family care. Such hopes, based on the proclivity of young people in the 1960s for collective forms of living, may be overly sanguine: much of the behaviour of the 1960s was narcissistic and self-indulgent. The conduct of many of second baby boomers during the 'selfish 1980s' was equally unencouraging.

Whatever the prospects for self-help, there is little reason to think that baby boomers will have no need of organised care in their old old age. It is commonly assumed that expectations will be high, to some extent governments of the 1980s and 1990s have encouraged this by effectively making the service user a consumer rather than a citizen (Deakin and Wright, 1990; Stewart and Walsh, 1992; Harden, 1993). However, the 'contract state' is by its nature unlikely to provide much space for the service user to participate in making decisions and choices about services, and in all probability it is this that baby boomers are most likely to want.

All the historical evidence we have indicates that the British population have been relatively modest in their expectations of state provision. They have not and are unlikely to expect palaces. On the other hand, they do not expect abuse either; in other words they want some assurance as to 'basic' quality. Quality is widely acknowledged to be the Achilles heel of markets, and, in the absence of nationally determined regulation, it remains to be seen how this aspect of care will unfold in the future. What will probably be different about future generations of older people is their desire to make their wishes known. They will expect to be 'empowered'. The extent to which service users have been 'empowered' in terms of being actively involved both in the process of assessment and in decisions about services at the individual level, and in strategic planning, through, for example, formal joint planning machinery (between health and social services), has varied widely since 1990. Even when procedures are put in place to secure participation by the user, it is by no means certain that circumstances will permit their participation on equal terms.

People needing care in the future will probably want things similar to those needing care now: the security of knowing that there will be help of a variety of kinds available, that it will be affordable, that it will be of at least reasonable quality and that they will have say in determining what they get. Despite aims to the contrary, there is some evidence that we are moving away from being able to offer today's older people these assurances, which does not augur well for the future.

■ Summary

- The main factor driving recent policy reform has been limited resources.

- Given the tension between resources and the much larger numbers of the baby boomers who may be in need:
  - it will tend to be cheaper and easier to provide whatever 'bulk' services are available than individually tailored care;
  - it is possible that 'warehousing' might return to the political agenda. This may occur despite the fact that the baby boomers may expect to be more 'empowered' than today's older people.

- Pressure on limited resources is leading to a narrower definition of need – linked to physical dependency and risk, in particular the availability of an informal carer. 'Need' is translating into those whom social services departments cannot ignore.

- The shift towards service provision based on market principles will result in more of the baby boomers having to pay for nursing home care and domiciliary services – leading to increasing inequality in access to these services.

- Baby boomers who do not meet the eligibility criteria for collectively provided care and cannot pay for it themselves run the risk of falling through the net.

6 Social care: today and beyond 2020

Maria Evandrou

The provision of health and social care to individuals with physical or mental impairments, or to frail older people, is a major social policy issue. Most social care for those in need of support is carried out in the community by family members. Demographic and socio-economic trends have heightened the pressure placed on the community to care for frail older people. At the same time, legislation has emphasised greater reliance on individuals and families to provide for those requiring support in old age. Some of the baby boomers can expect to be both *providers* of informal care and also, later in life, *recipients* of social care. However, it is not clear that the caring capacity attributed to 'the community' will be available in 2020 and beyond, and, furthermore, where it is available, whether it will match demand in terms of intensity and duration.

What are the expectations of the baby boomers both in terms of caring for frail family members and of being cared for by their family? Given the greater longevity of the baby boomers' parents (and grandparents), as well as improvement in their own and their partners' expectation of life, will the baby boomers as carers be faced with longer periods of caring? What is the likely impact of such caring work? As the baby boomers themselves age, will demand for informal care be higher in 2020 or will excess demand for care be soaked up by the private sector? Will today's children be willing or in a position to care for their baby boomer parents? What of the growing minority who will remain childless and not have this option? What future policies, in particular within social security and community care, should be adopted to support individuals with caring responsibilities? What will be the nature of the relationships and partnerships between the state, the family and the private sector, as employer and service provider?

This chapter attempts to shed light on these questions. It begins by investigating the role of family care within the broader context of current legislation. Evidence regarding who cares today and the level of service support that may be relied on is examined. We then turn to the impact of caring on economic and social well-being, both for those among the first baby boom cohort who are caring for dependent relatives today and for the informal carers of tomorrow. The balance between the likely demand for and the supply of informal care in 2020 is then evaluated, distinguishing the key determinants of demand and supply of social care. Finally, the major issues for the future for the family and government are discussed.

▬ The continuing importance of family care

Most social care provided in the community is by family members. In 1994, 93 per cent of all older people who had mobility problems and could not perform self-care tasks on their own, were helped by relatives or other household members; 71 per cent for bathing; 93 per cent for domestic tasks; and 85 per cent for walking outdoors (Figure 6.1). The importance of the role of the spouse or partner is obvious.

Who cares today?

In 1990, one person in seven (16 per cent) of the General Household Survey (GHS) sample was identified as having caring responsibilities for a sick, incapacitated or older person, of which about half provided regular support on their own; ie they were sole carers. Grossing up these figures nationally, they constitute *3.4 million sole carers* in Great Britain: *1.7 million* adults caring for someone within their own home, and another *1.7 million* people spending at least 20 hours per week providing care and support. Over one in ten of the 1990 GHS sample provided both personal and physical care, approximating to about 500,000 carers, who are involved in substantial levels of caring, for

Figure 6.1 Usual source of help for people aged 65 and over unable to do task by themselves, 1994

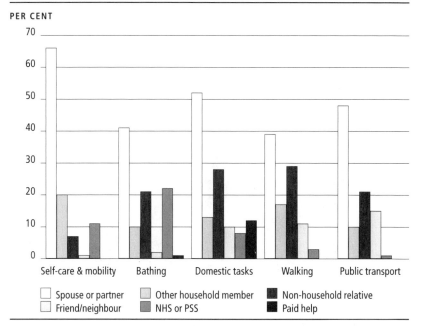

Source: GHS 1994. 'Self-care and mobility' includes getting around the house, getting to the toilet, in and out of bed, dressing and undressing and feeding. 'Bathing' includes bathing, showering and washing all over. 'Domestic tasks' includes shopping, dealing with personal affairs, washing dishes, cleaning windows, vacuuming, laundry, preparing food and drink and opening screwtops.

long hours and over lengthy periods. Among all carers, an average of 20 hours per week is spent performing caring tasks.

The proportion of adults reporting such caring responsibilities between 1985 and 1990 rose slightly (Figures 6.2a and 6.2b). Most of this rise is due to the increase in the proportion caring for dependants *outside* the household. The gender difference in the carers identified in the sample is small, 17 per cent of women compared to 14 per cent of men (Arber and Ginn, 1995). However, women carers are more likely to be caring for someone on their own, that is as *a sole carer* (ie 57 per cent versus 42 per cent), and for more hours per week. The nature of the caring work is different between male and female carers; female carers are more likely to provide *personal* care, whereas male carers are

Figure 6.2a Proportion of men (16 and over) who are carers, 1985–90

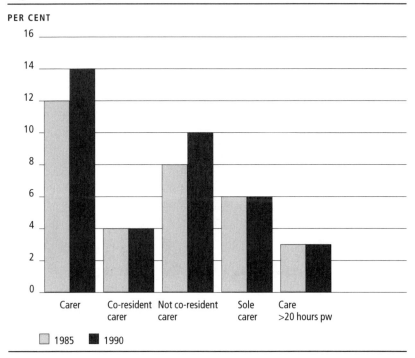

PER CENT

Source: GHS 1985, 1990.

more likely to provide support with *physical* tasks and *practical* help (Parker and Lawton, 1994). The age group most likely to be providing care includes the first baby boomers, ie those aged 45–59 years. One quarter of this age group report some form of caring responsibility. The likelihood of becoming a carer increases for women as they enter stages in their life course where their own children are older, in particular 16-plus, and also as they themselves get older. However, it is important to bear in mind that over a quarter of all informal carers (28 per cent) are aged 60 or over.

Carers supporting parents and parents-in-law (48 per cent) are most prevalent, a lower proportion caring for a spouse or child (16 per cent). Nearly three-quarters of carers (71 per cent) care for physically impaired dependants, 5 per cent support dependants with mental impairment, 17 per cent with both mental and physical impairments

Figure 6.2b Proportion of women (16 and over) who are carers, 1985–90

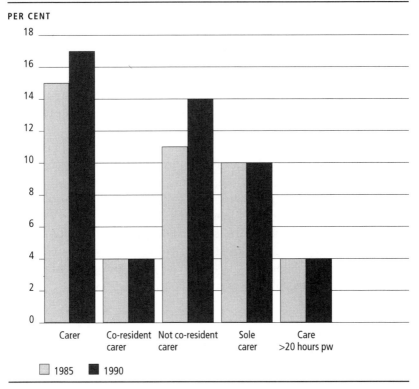

PER CENT

1985 ▢   1990 ■

Source: GHS 1985, 1990.

and 5 per cent with old age/other impairments. One-third of carers provide mainly personal or physical caring tasks.

Research using the 1985 GHS found that caring tends to be a longer-term experience, over four out of ten carers (42 per cent) reporting having cared for someone for between one and four years, and a fifth caring for a dependant for at least ten years. Only 12 per cent reported caring for less than one year (Evandrou, 1992, 1996).

The number of years that people will need care is likely to increase still further in the future as life expectancy increases. Parents and children will probably experience more than 50 years of overlapping adult life (Waerness, 1990). Baby boomers are more likely to have surviving parents than have earlier generations, and they are also more likely to have surviving grandparents at the same time that they are bringing up their children. Families may contain *two* generations of pensioners and perhaps even two generations of widows. For example, a member of the first baby boom at age 45 may have a youngest child aged 10, a parent (or parents) aged 70 and a grand-parent (or grandparents) aged 88, resulting in greater conflicting demands on the middle generations. The baby boomers will probably face multi- generational caring responsibilities, including their own children, parents and, for some, even grandparents. The caring experience in 2020 and beyond may be continuous, either sequential or simultaneous, over longer periods of time.

The length of time spent caring has implications as to the barriers to entering or re-entering the labour market for carers who wish to return to work, and also for the impact on the carers' quality of life, stress levels and general health status. Before looking at the effect of caring on the baby boomers' lives, it is useful to look briefly at what support they may be able to expect.

Government policy and current levels of formal support

With the family providing the bulk of support, informal carers are pivotal in maintaining disabled and frail people in the community. However, only recently have carers been formally placed in the policy arena. State service providers must now assess carers for community care support. Whilst the government White Paper *Caring for People* (Department of Health, 1989) places support for carers within state providers' responsibilities, the NHS and Community Care Act 1990 was silent on this. The Carers (Recognition and Services) Act 1995 redresses this somewhat. Under the 1995 Act, local authorities are obliged to carry out a separate assessment of the carer when assessing the cared-for-person for service support. Carers' views, their circumstances and their ability to continue providing care and support should be taken into account when the needs of the dependent person are reviewed and a care package is developed. The extent to which the

Act's implementation will constitute a real and continuing 'act of care' has been questioned (Clements, 1996). Given financial concerns, a key question is, will the assessments of carers contribute to higher levels of support or earlier intervention, and thus help relieve the pressures and workload? Or will it just add to the industry of needs assessment?

Respite care is not commonplace; over half (52 per cent) of all carers in the 1990 GHS reported that they had not had a break since caring responsibilities began. Providing consistent care with fewer breaks was found to be more prevalent among co-resident carers than other types of carers. So what other support services can informal carers rely on?

Support from the health and social services for the cared-for-person is generally limited. Fewer than half of the people being cared for received any health and social service support. Where they are receiving support, visits from a home help or a doctor are most common, followed by a district nurse. Service receipt fell between 1985 and 1990 for all services except for that of the district nurse, where it remained constant (Figure 6.3).

Figure 6.3 Percentage of dependants in receipt of social services, 1985–90

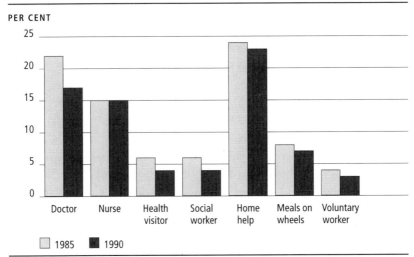

Source: GHS 1985 and 1990.

The 1990 GHS found that there was substantial variation in the services received by different types of carer (Table 6.1). People cared for by relatives in the *same* household are *less likely* to receive services (domestic, medical and personal care) than are other dependent individuals. The likelihood of provision was higher when the carer was a non-relative, irrespective of the dependency of the person being cared for and the caring relationship. Furthermore, home help services are more likely to be provided to women being cared for by men, rather than to men being cared for by women. In short, co-resident carers will probably receive a lower level of support than other types of carers, which may in turn have important implications for their levels of stress, general health status and quality of life.

In addition to receiving less formal support in future, carers and their dependants may increasingly find themselves having to pay for that support. As Jane Lewis discusses in Chapter 5, charging for home support services is emerging as *the* way to generate income and thus the central issue for local authorities having to implement community care reforms (Means and Smith, 1994).

Table 6.1 Receipt of social services by the dependant across different informal carers (%)

OF CARERS	Co-resident carer	Not co-resident carer	Sole carer	Caring for 50 or more hours per week	Caring for 20 or more hours per week
Doctor[a]	7	20	13	8	14
Nurse[a]	13	16	13	14	15
Health visitor[b]	2	5	3	2	3
Social worker[b]	2	5	3	4	3
Home help[b]	7	28	20	9	13
Meals on Wheels[b]	1	9	7	1	4
Voluntary worker	2	4	3	2	3
Other	6	12	10	11	10
(n)	(664)	(1944)	(1326)	(289)	(619)

a at least once in the last month
b more than once a month

Source: analysis of the GHS, 1990.

The Audit Commission reports that 'the discretionary framework for non-residential services has led to confusion with as many charging systems as there are local authorities' (Audit Commission, 1996). Of concern is the fact that individuals in very similar circumstances may be faced with different home care charges purely because the policies of their respective authorities vary. The success so far of income generation via charging remains unclear, as studies have shown that the amount of revenue obtained has tended to be very small; the proportion of home help expenditure covered by charges was 6 per cent in 1985/6 (Oldman, 1991). More recently, the Audit Commission (1996) has reported that income raised from charges totalled 9 per cent of the gross cost of services in 1992/3. Price may be a significant barrier to the use of services, deterring the poorer sections of the community who are in need of such support (Sinclair et al, 1990). Recent evidence from the Audit Commission survey of social services departments indicates that the impact charging has on users requires careful consideration; for example, in one particular social services department significant numbers of users of a home care service withdrew from the scheme when the previous flat-rate charge for everyone was replaced with a potentially more expensive system based on an assessed income scheme. Carers' financial positions may be affected by charging, especially when they provide support for dependants in the household where the joint financial resources are limited and precarious (Glendinning, 1990; Parker, 1990).

▪ The impact of caring

The experience of caring varies and informal carers themselves are a diverse group. There are both positive and negative aspects to caring and the caring relationship is essentially a changeable one. Many carers derive gratification and satisfaction at different stages of the caring relationship, and for varying lengths of time. Studies show that many carers successfully adjust to the caring role, taking on new or additional demands (Twigg, Atkin and Perring 1990; Parker 1990, 1993). High levels of stress among carers have been found to be combined with high levels of satisfaction, highlighting the dynamic nature of the relationship (Nolan and Grant, 1992; Grant and Nolan, 1993). Caring can have detrimental effects on one's economic, social and physical well-being. Of course, these effects are not mutually exclusive but interact, for example with health influencing the ability to accumulate resources and vice versa.

Economic impact

There are likely to be long-term as well as short-term economic effects on the baby boomers caring for someone, in terms of the impact on employment status, levels of earnings, savings and additional expenditure incurred from caring. As well as reduced *current* disposable income, reduced participation in the labour market and disrupted employment histories among carers, particularly women carers, may affect their economic status in their *own* old age in terms of income and pensions forgone, and lower earnings-related benefits in later life.

Research using the 1985 and 1990 GHSs shows that full-time employment rates for both male and female carers are lower than those of their non-carer counterparts (Evandrou and Winter, 1992; Evandrou, 1995). Carers are more likely to be employed in part-time jobs than are people without such caring responsibilities, standardising on gender and marital status. However, this tendency is restricted to women, as very few men work part-time, and is less marked for single women. In general, there is significant variation among different types of carers, the largest differentials in employment being found for co-resident or sole carers compared with non-carers.

Multivariate analysis taking into account age, socio-economic group, education, spouse's employment, age of the youngest child and ill-health using the 1990 GHS indicated that caring had an independent negative effect on employment for both men and women (Evandrou, 1995). The odds ratios indicate that a woman caring for an impaired person *inside* her household is only *half* as likely to be in full-time employment as her counterpart without such caring responsibilities and is *less* likely to be in part-time work. Women caring for dependants outside the home are three-quarters as likely to be in full-time employment than female non-carers, but are 30 per cent more likely to be in part-time work. The intensity of caring – ie the number of hours of care provided weekly – has the greatest impact on employment; women who are caring for over 50 hours per week are five times less likely to be in full-time employment than female non-carers. Furthermore, caring for a spouse or partner reduces the likelihood of paid work compared to caring for a parent or parent-in-law.

Carers' average weekly earnings were also found to be *below* that of non-carers, taking age and gender into account. In short, informal carers earn less on an hourly rate than non-carers. Co-resident carers and those caring for over 20 hours per week have markedly lower hourly rates of pay compared to non-carers, and also compared to carers caring for a dependant in their household (Evandrou, 1995). In addition to lower earnings, carers also experience, on average, lower net incomes than non-carers. This is despite the receipt of Invalid Care Allowance (ICA), which is seen by some as an alternative 'wage for caring'. Set at £37.35 per week, ICA is lower than the basic pension (£62.45) and Job Seekers Allowance (£49.15) (April 1997). For many carers, it clearly fails to provide any kind of earnings replacement.

In summary, carers' employment, earnings, hourly wage rates and income tend to be lower than their non-carer counterparts, standardising on age, gender and part-time/full-time work. However, the average picture masks enormous variation *among* different types of carers, reflecting the different demands various caring experiences place on individuals in terms of the labour market. It is questionable whether the existing welfare benefit system, specifically receipt of ICA, compensates carers' limited financial position sufficiently to place them on a par with their non-carer counterparts.

So far we have considered the impact on current economic position, but to what extent can informal carers expect to recover their economic welfare over their lifetime? Research elsewhere indicates that the lifetime impact on earnings and other income sources from caring remains (Evandrou and Falkingham, 1995). In particular, women with caring responsibilities face lower lifetime earnings and pension income than women on average, even after taking account of Home Responsibility Protection. Those women who care for five years or more have on average £13,000 (1985 prices) less lifetime earnings compared to all women. Furthermore, the state benefit system does not redress the position of carers in order to protect their lifetime living standards.

The health consequences of caring

Little is known nationally about the impact on carers' physical and mental well-being, in the short and the longer term, and how this interacts with carers' socio-economic positions. Research using the 1990 GHS (Evandrou, 1996) indicates that the self-reported health of carers as a whole is similar to that of non-carers, allowing for differences in age and gender. However, once the *level* of caring responsibilities and *intensity* of caring are distinguished, there is a significant relationship with 'not good' health in the last year: (1) caring for someone in the same home – especially one's spouse or partner; (2) bearing the main responsibility on one's own; (3) caring for someone with both physical and mental impairments; and (4) caring for over 50 hours per week. Multivariate analysis shows that, after taking into account a range of independent factors (including age, marital status, age of youngest child, own and spouse/partner's employment and educational level), caring for someone who is physically and mentally impaired has an effect on carers' own health; male carers are three-quarters as likely to be in good/fair health than men without such caring responsibilities, whilst female carers are four-fifths as likely.

Some carers are able to exercise a real choice between taking on caring and when to give it up. Those who experience poor health or long-term illness/disability are less likely to undertake caring initially than those in good health. However, *while* caring, carers faced with deteriorating health problems may discuss alternative care arrangements with their dependant and give up caring, compared with carers who continue to enjoy good health. Thus carers on average may report better general health, although for carers *within* and at different intensities of caring, poor general health is related to the experience of caring.

Social impact

Because time is a limited commodity, it is likely that the greater the time spent undertaking caring responsibilities, the less time will be available to spend in alternative ways. This may be especially true of carers who are combining their caring responsibilities with paid employment. A number of studies have found that people providing care may face reduced opportunities for pursuing hobbies and generally spend little time engaged in sports, relaxing, going on holiday or going for short breaks (Bowling, 1984; Wright, 1986; George and Gwyther, 1986; Qureshi and Walker, 1989; Clifford, 1990).

Over half of spouse carers (54 per cent) and nearly one in three carers who live with their dependant (28 per cent), had not spent *any* time in the previous year participating in sport *or* walking outdoors as a leisure activity. This compares with 18 per cent of non-carers (Figure 6.4). Furthermore, nearly three-quarters (71 per cent) of spouse carers had not participated in any physical leisure activity in the last month compared with their counterparts who had no such caring responsibilities (36 per cent). In addition, nearly four out of ten non-carers (39 per cent) had participated in at least one indoor activity in the previous month, compared with only 29 per cent of sole carers.

Other studies have found links between care provision, social isolation and poor health (Braithwaite, 1990; Parker, 1990). Restrictions on leisure activities, hobbies and general social participation is an

Figure 6.4 Proportion reporting having participated in outdoor activity in the last year by carer status (age–sex standardised)

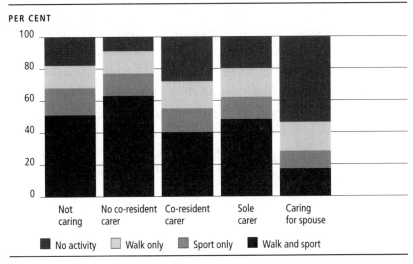

PER CENT

Source: GHS 1990.

important issue, especially as expectations of such activities at the relevant stage of the carer's life course may be very different. The social stimulation from paid employment is valued by many carers as much as the income generated from it (Stevenson, 1994). When carers are not in employment, access to respite and group support are as vital to the well-being of carers, especially for carers from black and minority ethnic communities where language barriers may be experienced (Baxter, 1988; McCalman, 1990). Enabling co-resident carers, and in particular sole co-resident carers, to participate in some activity outside the home should be a priority for providers of respite care. Yet it is precisely these groups of carers who are least likely to receive state service support.

■ The demand for social care in 2020 and beyond

Having looked at who cares today and considered the possible impact of caring, we are now at the position in 2020 when the second baby boom cohort will begin to retire and the first baby boomers will be in their mid-70s.

The demand for informal care in 2020 will reflect the following considerations:

- ■ Demographic factors – in particular the number of older people, which, as Chapter 1 shows, will be influenced by past trends in birth rate (most notably the timing of the baby boom cohorts), *and* trends in mortality.

- ■ Levels of dependency among the older population.

- ■ Social and cultural factors – especially social attitudes regarding expectations of family care provision.

- ■ Demand for alternative sources of care, whether local authority and private community care or institutional care. This in turn will be influenced by the availability of publicly provided care and the level of resources available to purchase alternative care.

Future levels of dependency

Chapter 1 presents data on the number of people who may need infor-mal care when the baby boom generations retire. However, the level of need for social care within these two groups will depend crucially on future trends in ill-health, both mental and physical. It could be argued that, having benefited from the NHS and having experienced improved living conditions in their youth and middle age, these post-war baby boomers will 'age healthily'. But Dunnell (1995), in a survey of trends in deaths, ill-health and health risk behaviours, found that, although almost universal improvements in death rates and increas-ing life expectancy might suggest that we are indeed healthier, trends in self-reported health status suggest there is *no* comparable general improvement in health. Life expectancy in old age has risen, but the extent to which these gains are disability-free is the subject of continu-ing debate (Grundy, 1992; Robine, Blanchet and Dowd 1992). Research indicates that, as life expectancy increases, there will be a rise in the proportion of people experiencing light to moderate disabilities but a fall in those with severe disabilities (Bone et al, 1995).

Trends presented in Chapter 4 suggest that younger generations report slightly *higher* levels of limiting long-standing illness than the previous generation at the same age; the good news is that, in terms of health risk behaviour, younger groups show lower levels of smoking than their elders. Over all, it is premature to assume that tomorrow's older people will be healthier than today's.

Preferred sources of support

Although there is no doubt that there will be more people, in terms of absolute numbers, requiring support in 2020 than today, it is less clear who will provide it and what mix of care the baby boomers them-selves will prefer. What will be the preferred sources of support among future older people?

Living with adult children in later life has not been popular historically; Qureshi (1996) cites Daniel Rogers who wrote as early as 1642 'no prison can be more irksome to a parent than a son or daugh-ter's house'. In a survey of residential preferences among the older population in the early 1980s, Thompson and West (1984) found moving in with relatives to be nearly as unpopular as entering an institution. There is no reason to suppose that the baby boomers will be any more inclined than previous generations to live with their children.

Co-residential care is only one form of informal care and in fact three-quarters of carers do not live with the person they are caring for. Nevertheless, there is evidence that older people would often prefer to rely on state services than on their children (Sixsmith, 1986; Siim, 1990). Janet Finch (1995), in her study of family obligations, reports that over one-third of respondents thought that children did not have an obligation to look after their parents. This was particularly true among elderly respondents – indicating that older people do not necessarily expect their children to care for them. Evidence from Norway indicates that between 1967 and 1989 there was a move away from relatives and towards formal agents as the preferred sources of support among older people (Daatland, 1990). Even if the baby boomers in retirement appear to favour formal rather than informal mechanisms for social care support, the key question is whether the level and range of such support will be available and, if so, whether they will be expected to, or even able to, pay for such services.

There is a degree of complementarity and substitutability among the public, private and informal care sectors. If less publicly provided care is available, or used, this may stimulate demand for informal or privately financed care. Jane Lewis, in Chapter 5, assesses what the baby boomers may expect in the form of community care in 2020. One of the main trends is the increase in likelihood, and the level, of charges being levied on whatever services are available.

Ability to pay for care

The ability of the baby boomers to pay for care will depend on their previous employment experiences and the accumulation of pension entitlements and other assets to secure an adequate income in later life. The conclusions of Chris Phillipson and Ruth Hancock in Chapters 2 and 3 are that some of the baby boomers *will* be in a position to purchase care, but some *will not*. There has been a trend towards earlier withdrawal from the labour market and younger generations of men both enter the labour market later and leave earlier, and also have lower overall participation rates at any given age. Thus the second baby boomers will have fewer years of working life over which to accumulate reserves. But membership of occupational pension schemes has risen with time within cohorts, and younger cohorts have a higher membership rate for a given age. Younger generations of men and women are also much more likely to have a private pension. Those who are members of such schemes may find themselves with higher levels of disposable income in later life than have today's older population.

However, the second baby boom generation faced particularly high unemployment levels when they began to enter the labour market, compared with the first baby boom, and this may disadvantage some of them in their adult working life and also in their expectations and the building up of resources. It is likely that there will be a greater degree of inequality in later life within the baby boom cohorts, and especially among the younger cohort, than among today's older population. In order to protect people who will not be in a position to finance their long-term care needs, the Joseph Rowntree *Inquiry into Meeting the Costs of Continuing Care* proposed a national care insurance scheme. Contributions would be compulsory, and for those whose contributions were insufficient to cover the full cost of their care the balance would be met from public funds (Diba, 1996). This would ensure free social care at the point of delivery for all older baby boomers, regardless of their resources.

▪ The supply of social care in the future

The supply of informal care in 2020 and beyond is largely a function of present and future demographic trends, and in particular the patterns of family formation and dissolution among the baby boom generations. The supply of potential carers will be influenced by the existence of kin, marriage patterns, the number of children, trends in household composition and family relations.

Availability of spouses to care

By far the most important source of practical and emotional support is one's spouse or partner (see Figure 6.1). Predicting the marital status of baby boomers in later life is complex. Improved death rates at older ages will mean that fewer older people in the twenty-first century are likely to be widowed. However, death is not the only way in which marriages are dissolved, and rising divorce rates may more than offset the fall in widowhood.

Jane Falkingham in Chapter 1 informs us that recent family formation patterns indicate:

- a shift towards later marriage;

- a higher proportion of second baby boom will remain unmarried;

- greater proportions of 75-year-old first baby boomers will be living in single-person households than in previous generations;

- it is likely that this proportion will be even greater among the second baby boomers.

Trends in partnership indicate that more people in the future will be living 'solo' – primarily because they have never married or have separated or divorced. Fewer baby boomers will be living in a union with a spouse or partner, indicating a fall in the potential supply of informal care from spouses/partners.

Trends in the 'availability' of children

Children are also an important source of social care. As Figure 1.1 shows, since the peak in 1964 the overall birth rate has decreased. This trend has important ramifications for the baby boomers in later life, as it suggests that both cohorts will have, on average, fewer children than their predecessors. This is reflected in the rise in the social care dependency ratio, ie the number of people aged 75 years and over per woman aged 45–59 years (see Figure 1.4).

However, a lower birth rate does not necessarily mean that there will be fewer children to provide support for the baby boomers in later life. In terms of the potential support for older people from their children, it is whether you have *any* children at all rather than the number of children that is of central importance (Knodel, Knapaporn and Siriboon, 1992). Several studies have shown that the responsibility for providing care tends to be assumed by one child, rather than shared among siblings (Kendig, 1986; Kendig, Hashimoto and Coppard, 1992). Thus, if a lower birth rate has been achieved through reductions in the number of children per union rather than an increase in the proportion who never have a child, the implications for future levels of support will be different. The proportion of each cohort remaining childless at old age is a key variable.

Figure 1.7 shows the proportion of women from the second baby boom who have never had a child by a particular age. By the age of 25 only 37 per cent of the women born in 1946 had not given birth, whereas 60 per cent of those born in 1964 were still childless at the same age. If this trend continues, over one-fifth (21 per cent) of the second baby boomers will remain childless. On this basis, therefore, it is likely that we shall see a decline in the potential supply of informal care from their children.

There has also been a rise in divorce and remarriage. An increase in 'reconstituted families' may mean that, although there are fewer natural children, there may be *more* children over all per parent, ie both natural and step-children. Little is known about how divorce may affect family ties and feelings of inter-generational obligation. Will children of divorced parents, and in particular of fathers who failed to maintain regular contact with them, show the same willingness to care? Similarly, will ex-daughters-in-law be prepared to offer care to their ex-mother- and father-in-law? Evidence from the USA shows that adults who had experienced marital disruption themselves provided less help to elderly parents than did those with intact marriages (Cicirelli, 1983). There is no evidence to date on whether the *children* of divorced parents will also exhibit the same tendency towards their parents.

Traditionally the caring relationship has been that of parent–child. Now the role of grandparent–grandchild is attracting increasing attention. As Jerrome (1996) points out, given increased life expectancy, this relationship can now last for many decades, perhaps even as long as 50 years. At present, adult grandchildren are not reported as playing a significant role in the care of their grandparents (Qureshi, 1996); but with the growing proportion of grandchildren who will experience the divorce of their parents, this may change in the future. Certainly, we are seeing the emergence of increasingly complex family structures, and new forms of family ties. Janet Finch (1995) concludes that family responsibilities today are based on 'individual "commitments" rather than on "fixed obligations" associated with a genealogical link . . . this means that filial responsibilities cannot be relied upon as the basis for the [future] provision of care'.

Economic, social and cultural factors affecting the supply of informal care

The presence or absence of kin is not the only factor affecting the possible supply of informal care. The willingness and ability to provide care will depend on social attitudes and expectations regarding the provision of care, alternative employment opportunities open to potential carers, migration patterns and geographic mobility, and the proximity of the older person to relatives. In all of these, the baby boomers are likely to experience circumstances different from those of today's older population.

Both daughters and daughters-in-law have been shown to be less likely to provide assistance to older relatives if they are in full-time work (Qureshi and Walker, 1989). If current trends continue, women will have longer working lives and spend more time in full-time employment. Thus fewer women may be in a position to be available for informal care, and, if they are, they may be available only for shorter periods of time or less intense caring responsibilities depending on their work commitments.

Not surprisingly, geographic proximity has been found to be a key factor in determining whether family care is offered (Warnes and Ford, 1996). Wenger (1992) has argued that 'out-migration' will have substantial effects on the supply of informal care. More of the baby boomers will have moved during their lifetimes, in search of jobs and for other reasons. We are beginning to witness international commuting with improvements in travel time, such as the channel tunnel and inter-city air shuttle services. Greater mobility among the first and second baby boom generations and among their children may mean that fewer will have kin living nearby.

In conclusion, the combined effect of complex family structures, increased participation by women in the labour market, greater geographic mobility and migration is likely to shrink the potential pool of informal carers in 2020 and beyond. This may in turn place greater pressure on the demand for formal care services. Meanwhile, the supply of state-provided health and social services is likely to decrease further unless there is a change in political commitment and public expenditure. Private sector provision of both residential and nursing home care will continue to expand and soak up some of the increase in demand. However, a significant minority of the older baby boomers in the twenty-first century will not be in a position to purchase the care they need. For the one-fifth of second baby boomers who will be childless, unless they are able to finance social care in their old age, the options look bleak.

▬ Issues for social care policy in 2020

Future policy regarding social care in the twenty-first century should take on board a number of issues:

- Policies regarding cash benefits and services at national and local levels need to reflect the diversity of caring experiences and the socio-economic position of carers and of the people being cared for.

- In 2020 there will be greater ethnic diversity among the older population than is the case today.

- Community services should be accessible, flexible and responsive to the needs of the carer and their dependant.

- Services should include respite options that are offered within or near to the carer's home, neighbourhood-based care schemes, as well as information, advice and carers' network support. Choice and control should be explicit elements within the care system planned.

- Greater involvement of carers and dependants in the planning and the evaluation of community care support should be fostered.

- Flexible employment options and 'family-friendly' employment policies and practices that facilitate people combining paid work with care responsibilities should be encouraged.

- Current benefit levels for carers do not provide an adequate replacement income that recognises both the short-term and the longer-term economic impact of caring. There is a need for a benefit that both provides an appropriate 'wage' *and* protects their lifetime living standards.

Informal carers may be faced with both a lower income in their own old age, owing to interrupted paid employment, and the possibility of poorer health. These may in turn result in greater demand for health and social services in the twenty-first century. Developing policies of ongoing support for carers may mitigate the costs of tomorrow's dependants.

Carers' needs and rights have begun to be formally acknowledged within the new procedures for care management and assessment, reinforced by the Carers Act 1995. This is vitally important in recognising the significant contribution made by informal carers in Britain. However, *recognition* of carers' needs does not necessarily translate into *meeting* carers' needs. Given the concerns about the extent of community care funding, it remains to be seen whether the policy statements will materialise in any effective support, reducing the workload of carers.

■ Summary

- Baby boomers are more likely to have surviving parents and grandparents than have earlier cohorts. As such, they may face multi-generational caring responsibilities, in addition to bringing up their own children.

- Time spent caring has implications for the carers' economic resources, quality of life, stress levels and general health.

- The health and social services support received by the cared-for person is generally limited, and has fallen over time. If current policies continue, baby boomers who care for a frail older relative in the future may expect even lower levels of state support and face growing charges for that support. Private provision of domiciliary care services will increase.

- The *demand* for informal care in 2020 and beyond will be a function of:
  - future levels of dependency;
  - preferred sources of support;
  - the ability to pay for alternative sources of social care.

- The *supply* of informal care in 2020 and beyond will be a function of:
  - the marital status of older people;
  - the number of kin and their availability and willingness to provide care. This will be affected by social attitudes regarding care provision, employment opportunities open to potential carers, migration patterns and the proximity of the older baby boomer to relatives.

- In 2020 and beyond, when the baby boomers themselves are older, it is likely that demand for informal care will outstrip supply.

- For the one-fifth of the second baby boomers who will be childless, unless they are able to finance social care in their old age, the options look bleak.

- Future policies should reflect the diversity of informal carers' experiences, encourage family-friendly employment practices, and provide an adequate income and long-term financial protection.

▪ Acknowledgement

I am indebted to the ESRC Data Archive, University of Essex, and to the Office of National Statistics for making the General Household Survey data available for analysis.

7 Housing options in 2020: a suitable home for all?

Robin Means

This chapter considers the likely housing of baby boomers when they retire. Earlier chapters have indicated the importance of one's housing history and current housing situation in determining standards of living and choices in later life. Ruth Hancock in particular, in Chapter 3, considers issues of inheritance in terms of financial resources and the potential of home equity release as a way for people to pay for their care packages.

This chapter focuses more directly on housing itself. It considers the increase in owner-occupation in later life and analyses the implications of this for housing needs in 2020, perhaps requiring more flexible housing options to meet those needs. The second half of the chapter considers the situation of older people who will have continued to live in rented accommodation. From the outset, however, it must be recognised that housing policy in Britain is driven not by a desire to respond to the needs of groups such as older people but by concerns about the relation of housing to the broader economy (Maclennan, 1994). Thus, increases or decreases in the interest rates charged by building societies on mortgages are seen by government as a mechanism for deflating or inflating the economy. An inability to sell one's house or to afford one in the south of England can be seen as a source of labour market rigidity, and hence an obstacle to economic growth. The mushrooming cost of housing benefit is seen by many as central to the fiscal crisis of welfare and the resulting growth in public sector borrowing (Kemp, 1994).

■ More than bricks and mortar

This chapter is about much more than the provision of bricks and mortar for the baby boomers when they reach old age. Older people need appropriate and affordable accommodation, but they also need a home, a place where they can feel relaxed and secure and where they can surround themselves with personal possessions. A home provides privacy, familiarity and independence (Higgins, 1989; Gurney and Means, 1993; Langan, Means and Rolfe, 1996). It should be remembered that community care policy in Britain is based, in part, on the belief that frail older people prefer to live in ordinary housing rather than in institutions, because the former has a far greater capacity than the latter to be a home.

From this perspective, a crucial issue for 2020 is how housing can be developed for older people in a way that maximises their ability to make a genuine home in whatever accommodation option they choose. The key issue that must be addressed in this context is the relationship of home to attachments to certain houses because of the memories and emotions that they provoke. Over 30 years ago, Peter Townsend (1963) spoke of how:

> Home was the old armchair by the hearth, the creaky bedstead, the polished lino with its faded pattern, the sideboard with its picture gallery, and the lavatory with its broken latch reached through the rain. It embedded a thousand memories and held promise of a thousand contentments. It was an extension of personality.

More recently, Harrison and Means (1990) discovered similar sentiments from the older owners who were using the services of Care and Repair and Staying Put home improvements agencies. The critical issue is the extent to which such powerful feelings about specific houses will continue to be a key factor for older people in 2020. Will the baby boomers be more used to moving and recreating a home? Do older tenants have the same positive feelings about their accommodation, especially if they have lived in the same home for a very long period? How can the 'moving-on' housing options of the future help older people re-establish their sense of home?

■ Baby boomers in 2020 – tenure projections

It is, of course, impossible to predict with certainty the exact tenure profile by age that will exist in 2020. The driving factor will almost certainly be the 'roll-on' effect of present tenure battles, but this process will be mediated by supply and demand factors in the intervening period. Individuals can choose or be forced to leave one tenure for another, and governments can try to influence this process by increasing the attractiveness of some housing options over others.

It is known that, although today's older people are less likely to be owner-occupiers than those in middle age, there has been a growth in owner-occupation in later life that has paralleled the growth of owner-occupation more generally in British society (Figure 7.1). Projections confirm that the process will continue into the next century as the first baby boomers, at present middle aged, take their owner-occupation with them into later life. Such levels of home ownership are projected to reach 66 per cent by 2001, and to cover 3.8 million households headed by someone over 60 of whom one-third will be over 75 years of age (Rolfe, Mackintosh and Leather, 1993). By 2020, when the second baby boomers begin to retire, ownership levels among those over 60 will be even greater.

Figure 7.1 Ownership rates by age of head of household; Great Britain, 1975–91

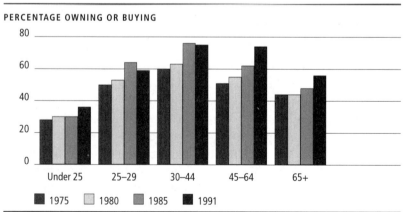

Source: Rolfe, Mackintosh and Leather (1993).

Although renting is already the minority tenure of later life, there are still more older people in housing association, local authority and private rented accommodation than the rest of the adult population: the 1991 Census indicated that households with a head over 60 occupied 46 per cent of council houses and 44 per cent of housing association properties, and the 'old old' (ie those over 75 years) are heavily represented in the private unfurnished accommodation sector. The projection of these trends through to 2020 is extremely difficult because they depend heavily on the presence or absence of government support for socially rented housing and for private rented housing. It seems highly likely, however, that a sizeable rental sector will still exist in 2020, and that older households will continue to be 'over-represented' in such accommodation.

Sheltered housing is often seen as synonymous with housing for older people but only a small percentage of older people have ever lived in such accommodation. Tinker et al (1994) have estimated that about 9 per cent of older households within the community live in some form of sheltered housing, and that in 1992 there were just under half a million sheltered housing units in England. The next twenty-five years are unlikely to see any major expansion in overall numbers. The sheltered housing for sale sector suffered major reverses during the last recession and is only just beginning to show significant signs of recovery. The Housing Corporation (1996) is increasingly reluctant to make sheltered housing schemes for rent a priority for development by housing associations. However, sheltered housing will remain important, especially in the eyes of policy makers, because of its potential contribution to the housing of frail older people, and hence a reduction in their need to enter expensive residential care.

Having discussed the likely tenure breakdown in 2020, it is now necessary to consider the key housing issues the baby boomers will face in each tenure and the housing options that need to be developed. Before doing this, one final point needs to be made in this section. Unless there are dramatic changes in government policy over the next twenty-five years, all tenures will be bedevilled by poor housing conditions. In *Papering over the Cracks*, Leather, Mackintosh and Rolfe (1994) reviewed the present situation and concluded that:

- One in 13 homes in the UK is unfit to be lived in.
- Problems of dampness, condensation and mould growth are widespread.
- The backlog of comprehensive repairs to privately owned homes is at least £70 billion at 1994 prices.

A significant proportion of baby boomers are already victims of such terrible housing conditions.

▪ Older owner-occupiers: issues and options in 2020

Debates about owner-occupation in later life have tended to focus on the struggles of people on low and middle incomes to repair and maintain their homes. One response to this has been the growth of agencies such as the Care and Repair and Staying Put projects, which advise older owners on home improvement and adaptation (Leather and Mackintosh, 1992). The work of some voluntary organisations includes helping older people to repair or maintain their homes. Older owners have been seen as requiring specialist help to understand and follow through the home improvement process, including advice on how to fund such work with grants and from private finance. A second linked response has been the debate about the need for improved home equity release mechanisms. Much has been written on the 'house rich, cash poor' who cannot afford to look after their property despite being outright owners and thus having considerable assets tied up in the house (Bull and Poole, 1989). The problem has been, and continues to be, how to release that wealth without selling the house.

Debates on owner-occupation in later life need to broaden out from this agenda in the coming years if appropriate housing options are to be developed for older owner-occupiers. A number of factors support this view. First, there is evidence that the nature of repair and maintenance problems faced by older owner-occupiers as a whole is becoming more similar to that faced by the rest of the owning population. Compared to the 1986 Survey (Department of the Environment, 1988), the 1991 English House Condition Survey (Department of the

Environment, 1993) suggested that the home disrepair problems of older households, especially those in the 60–74 age group, were not much greater than those of many younger owners. It is hard to be certain why this is so, but it might indicate that owner-occupation is a problematic tenure for two main groups – those on low income (including older people) and those in poor health (most of whom will be over 75 years of age). Research by Gibbs (1993) has complicated this picture by estimating from analysis of the 1986 and the 1991 House Condition Surveys that only 6 per cent of older households are 'house rich, cash poor' compared to more than half who are both house poor and cash poor. If we project this situation on another twenty-five years, we see a sizeable group of owners entering later life in a situation where they have long struggled to cope as owners, because of their low incomes, their long periods of unemployment and their disrupted personal histories (see Chapters 2 and 3). Such people may be vulnerable owners in 2020, but their vulnerability was established long before later life. However, in emphasising this narrowing of experience, it should be remembered that single older people, especially women, and the 'old old' remain two of the worst-housed groups of owners.

Second, the image of the vulnerable older owner must be broadened out from that of someone who has lived in the same terraced or semi-detached property most of their life. It should be recognised that housing options will be needed for many middle class professionals, who were once expected to retire with a good occupational pension and a detached house in suburbia. Yet the late 1980s and early 1990s saw a massive shake-out of middle-aged middle managers from the first baby boom cohort, many of whom will never be able to re-establish the old certainties of steady job and promotion (Hutton, 1994). What all this will mean for older people in twenty-five years' time is difficult to unravel, but it suggests that many may enter later life with considerable debt as the consequence of their attempts to maintain middle-class lifestyles and middle-class housing.

Third, we need to question the assumption that nearly all older owners will continue to be outright owners, because a growing percentage may well continue to have mortgage commitments. Later marriages, later childbirth, higher divorce and remarriage rates and the temptation to take out second or even third mortgages may begin to paint a rather different picture of the older owner than the one that prevails at the moment. Indeed Ruth Hancock, in Chapter 3, suggests that nearly a third of owner-occupiers aged 65–74 in 2011 will still have a mortgage. Such mortgages need not be a problem if incomes are able to cover such expenses but one suspects that many individuals will find themselves in difficult personal circumstances.

Fourth, the repair and maintenance needs of older owners need to be recognised as much wider than the classic issues of electrical wiring, damp proofing and leaking roofs and windows. Older people are often equally concerned about issues of how to heat their homes efficiently and how to maintain their gardens as frailty increases, while burglary and home security are major concerns to many (Langan, Means and Rolfe, 1996). For older people on very low incomes, repairs and replacing locks following burglary can be problematic, especially if they lack insurance cover. Worries about such issues can undermine the sense of one's home as a secure place and hence precipitate entry into sheltered housing and residential care. Some home improvement agencies have started to respond to this situation by obtaining grants to enable them to offer home security services, insulation packages and advice on energy efficiency (Means et al, 1994).

Fifth, the weakness of the discussion so far is that it reinforces the view of older people as hapless victims unable to cope with the pressures of modern life. It must be remembered that the vast majority of older people enjoy their homes and many take considerable pleasure in their ability to maintain them to a high standard. Later life can bring increased leisure time (Laslett, 1989) and hence the prospect of improving the garden, the home decoration and the general appearance of the house. In this respect, it is crucial to remember that it is the baby boom cohorts who have been at the heart of the 'do it yourself' revolution within which the development of a wide range of household maintenance skills has been both a shared hobby with partners and often an economic necessity. Hedges and Clemens (1994) organised a survey on the housing attitudes of over 3000 owners and tenants for the Department of the Environment. Table 7.1 is taken from their work, and emphasises the depth of 'do it yourself' skills across tenures and across age groups. Many of these households will have

Table 7.1 Self-assessed ability to do DIY work, by age (%)

TASK	16–24	25–34[a]	35–44	45–54[b]	55–64	65–74	75+
Change a fuse	98	97	98	97	92	81	56
Install electric socket	35	52	52	57	43	33	14
Change tap washer	72	81	83	83	71	60	37
Wall paper	84	90	90	90	77	63	28
Pane of glass	43	64	69	70	55	42	20
Average no. of tasks	4.2	4.7	4.8	4.8	4.1	3.5	1.8
Base number	185	620	616	559	442	473	373

a Includes the second baby boom.
b Includes the first baby boom.

Source: Hedges and Clemens (1994).

the resources to pursue a lifestyle that places a high emphasis upon improving the home.

Finally, a crucial issue for older people concerns their need to consider whether their home needs to change or if they need to change home in response to their evolving needs in later life. The advantages and disadvantages of staying put versus moving comprise a constant theme in the housing literature, and will remain a practical concern to the older baby boomers in the twenty-first century. Below are listed some of the changing needs that might emerge, and how these might be responded to whether by staying put in one's present home or by moving on to a new one.

Lifestyle aspirations in retirement For people wishing to stay put, life in retirement can involve seeking membership of new clubs (bowls, bridge, embroidery etc) but others prefer the more dramatic choice of migration to a favoured locality such as Devon or Cornwall. As more of the baby boomers will have taken foreign holidays than previous cohorts, this might even include moving abroad.

Loneliness This is a big issue for many, especially after bereavement, and can lead to an effort to increase friendship networks locally. For others it precipitates moves to be nearer relatives and, in some cases, the building of an annexe (often called a 'granny flat') onto a relative's house. As Maria Evandrou discusses in Chapter 8, the baby boomers may also be able to access friendship networks across the information super-highway.

Home security As already indicated, one response is to improve the safety of one's home through burglar alarms, window locks and perhaps – by the time the baby boomers retire – closed-circuit TV, but another is to move to a safer neighbourhood or housing environment. Fears about security of the home may be of greater importance in future if crime increases. Alternatively, the baby boomers who have already grown up with house and car alarms may see it less as a problem of old age and more as a way of life.

Money shortages For people in more expensive property, 'trading down' to release income is an option, although Rolfe, Leather and Mackintosh (1993) warn that specialist options such as bungalows and sheltered housing are expensive to buy and rarely leave much capital over for re-investment by the mover. The alternative is to stay put and to take out a home income plan, which is really a loan taken out, using one's home as guarantee of repayment, whereby an agreed sum is paid to the older person, usually on a monthly basis. The Bank of Scotland has recently developed a 'shared appreciation mortgage', in which no monthly interest repayments are required; when the home covered by this mortgage is sold, the loan is repaid together with an agreed percentage of the increase in the value of the home.

Concern about future health and mobility This can lead to a decision to move to a bungalow, to private sheltered housing or to accommodation nearer shops and other community facilities. Equally, it can result in adaptation of the existing accommodation to prepare for future health and mobility needs.

Deteriorating health and mobility Here the 'move on' options begin to include moving in with relatives (perhaps into an annexe) or even entry into residential and nursing home care. For people determined or forced to stay put, further redesign of the home may have to be considered, including very specific adaptations ranging from grab rails to the installation of a downstairs bathroom. Such adaptations may require the owner to explore whether they are entitled to help from the at present mandatory, but means-tested, disabled facilities grant (Mackintosh and Leather, 1994).

Deteriorating fabric of the house This was the focus of the earlier discussion on repair and maintenance. In terms of options to stay put or move on, it must be recognised that an alternative to repair of one's present home is to move to more manageable accommodation. This might be a smaller property, a move to renting or possibly to some form of mixed, shared or flexible tenure in which one becomes part owner and part renter (Ayrton et al, 1990; Oldman, 1990).

The above list gives not only an indication of the dilemmas, problems and challenges that will be faced by the older owner-occupiers of the baby boom generations but also begins to spell out some of the options that might be available. They are presented in Table 7.2 with an outline of possible difficulties in achieving the options.

Rolfe, Leather and Mackintosh (1993) reviewed the strengths and weaknesses of existing options, especially with regard to tackling the main housing problems of people on low and middle incomes. Their conclusions are depressing in that few fully workable solutions were found (Table 7.2). In addition to problems already discussed in this chapter, they were critical of growing restrictions on the availability of home improvement grants and pessimistic about the capacity of existing home income plans or equity release schemes to generate significant additional income for older owner-occupiers.

The rest of this section offers suggestions for positive ways forward for ensuring the emergence of housing options appropriate to the needs of older owner-occupiers in 2020. The first point to stress is that to move or to stay is a complex decision, and improved information and advice should be developed for older people on what their realistic options might be. Any assessment of this key decision in later life must involve an awareness of the possibilities for improving the quality of life within the existing home and the possibilities for achieving this through a move. Such advice must recognise and take account of the emotions of the older person about their present home. It must also be hard-headed about the drawbacks as well as the opportunities offered by a move in terms of such issues as cost (eg service charges in

Table 7.2 Options and problems for low and middle income elderly owners

Group	Problems	Options	Difficulties in achieving options
Low and middle income home owners with low home equity	Low income Limited equity Some households in poor conditions Dwelling too large Dwelling inaccessible	Move to local authority or housing association Improve/adapt home Trade down Move to private sheltered housing	Limited availability of tenancy Erosion of housing equity Loss of entitlement to benefits Unlikely to be able to trade down Limited availability of renovation grants Absence of equity release mechanisms
Low and middle income home owners with a higher level of home equity	Some households in poor conditions Dwelling too large Dwelling inaccessible	Move to local authority or housing association Improve/adapt home Trade down Move to private sheltered housing	Limited availability of tenancy Erosion of housing equity Limited scope to trade down Limited availability of renovation grants Absence of equity release mechanisms

Source: Rolfe, Leather and Mackintosh (1993, p 84).

private sheltered schemes) and other limitations (eg is your chosen option going to work as your health deteriorates?). Such advice has to be neutral and not tied to a particular provider product, such as the sale of private sheltered housing units. It can be argued that the idea of a national network of housing advice is 'pie in the sky', because advice agencies could not survive on fee income for advice and would be unlikely to attract sufficient public subsidy. However, such a network was a central recommendation of the Commission on Family Housing (1994) working group on housing older people, which was supported by the European Commission.

A possibility is that home improvement agencies such as Care and Repair and Staying Put projects might be able to perform this advice and organisational role (Harrison and Means, 1993), but the criteria of neutrality would be met only if they were not committed to 'selling' staying put options. Fletcher and Herbert (1996) have suggested the need to develop local service networks from which neutral advice and information could be obtained on a wide range of housing, care and support services available from accredited providers. A slightly different approach is to increase the capacity of older people to advise themselves through the development of a self-administered housing option appraisal system along the lines proposed by Heywood (1993). It is clear that any improved advice network must be backed up by mechanisms that will protect older people from the danger of choosing housing options that are exploitative. There continues to be enormous concern about unreasonable leasehold conditions that some older people are expected to sign when buying a property in a sheltered housing scheme (Miller, 1994).

It is clear that most older people will decide to stay put if their general maintenance, home security, repair or adaptation needs can be responded to (McCafferty, 1996). This suggests the desirability of a national network of home improvement agencies that can support and advise older people through this process. However, such agencies require the back-up of government policies on home improvement, home security, energy efficiency and home adaptation to ensure that agency staff can organise an appropriate response. Good advice is no good if the agreed housing option cannot then be delivered. In terms of home adaptation, this occurs almost despite the bewildering complexity of relationships between grant officers, occupational therapists and technical officers (Heywood, 1994), and this suggests the need for a more coherent and less complex system for processing applications for the disabled facilities grant. The previous system was based on both means-tested mandatory grants for major renovations (with a maximum grant level of £20,000 in England and £24,000 in Wales) and a discretionary grant for minor works available to owners receiving means-tested benefits. However, the Housing Grants, Construction and Regeneration Act 1996 has abolished mandatory renovation grants, and there are thus fears of a further deterioration in the housing stock and possible 'knock on' effects for poor older owners. Against this, discretionary grants for minor works are now available to anyone over 60 and to disabled people, not just to those receiving means-tested benefits.

A detailed blueprint for sustainable housing renewal policies can be found in *Papering over the Cracks* by Leather, Mackintosh and Rolfe (1994). The proposed strategy is based on the belief that 'while the responsibility for the repair, improvement and maintenance of private properties rests primarily with the owners, it should be the responsibility of government to take active steps to promote and encourage housing renovation and to provide help to those who cannot afford to do so'. They argue that, in the likely absence of higher levels of public spending, the maximum grant should be lowered so that available public expenditure can be spread more widely, that areas of greatest need should be targeted and that a greater emphasis on loans should be introduced. For people on low incomes, they call for new loan systems under which repayment costs can be deferred or reduced. These include:

- Equity-sharing loans under which households receive a loan for repair but assign a share of the value of their house to the lender.

- Department of Social Security help with interest payments.

- Rolled-up interest loans or reverse-mortgages on which repayments of capital are deferred.

- Mortgage benefits payments along the lines proposed by Webb and Wilcox (1991) for house purchase but extended to house repair.

The approach outlined by Leather and colleagues emphasises the responsibilities of the home owner as well as the responsibilities of government. The cumulative impact of a failure to repaint the house, repair the guttering etc can be more serious renovation problems in the future. Because buying a house is an act of private consumerism, owner-occupiers have to recognise that it is in their interests to maintain it as much as they do their motor car. Failure to do so can endanger not only the 'health' of the house but also unwitting future owners who buy these accumulated problems from the previous vendor. Leather, Mackintosh and Rolfe (1994) lament the 'widespread lack of public awareness of the need for carrying out repair and maintenance work and a lack of knowledge about how to get work done properly'. They call not only for public awareness campaigns backed up by other practical measures such as adult education courses and free or low cost help in identifying problems but also for a consideration of whether vendors should be made more responsible for latent property defects.

However, Leather and colleagues recognise that such an overall approach may work for owners on middling incomes but remain unworkable for those on very low or very uneven incomes. Thus a third area requiring development is better options for escaping or partially escaping owner-occupation for baby boomers who may be in this situation. Opportunities for transfer into socially rented housing need to be increased, as does the range of shared, mixed or flexible tenure schemes that are available to older people. However, the research of Oldman (1990) reveals that such schemes are vulnerable to changes in housing benefit regulations, so enthusiasm for their growth has to be tempered until it is clear that they can offer the level of financial security required by low income older owners who are interested in moving into some kind of part own/part rent arrangement.

Finally, there is a need for private developers to build homes to higher access standards so that houses become far more flexible for the changing needs of their inhabitants. For example, a rethinking of the location of light switches, electrical plug points etc could help to make houses far less of a problem to people as soon as they start to experience frailty. The Access Committee for England has carried out detailed work on the specific issue of mobility (Brewerton and Darton, 1997) and has argued that all new domestic housing should be built to the following standards:

- The approaches and entrances to dwellings should be accessible to disabled people.

- Areas normally used by visitors such as hall, toilet and living rooms should be accessible to disabled people, including wheelchair users.

- Dwellings on more than one storey or level should be designed internally for easy movement and be amenable to modification, if necessary, for people of limited mobility.

In terms of design criteria this means, for example, that 'wherever possible there should be a level or gently sloping path, with a maximum gradient of 1 in 20 from the adapted footway to the door of the dwelling'. The Access Committee concluded that such specifications should be included within building regulations because 'the advantages of access through regulation for developers and designers is the degree of certainty and the knowledge that they will be universally applied'. The Department of the Environment (1995) has produced a Consultation Paper proposing improved standards for access to the entrance halls and the toilets of new residential homes. It is argued that this would enable more disabled people to visit friends and also help people with reduced mobility to 'stay put' in their own home. Despite the positive reaction to the Consultation Paper, no attempt has yet been made to implement its proposals.

Baby boomer renters : issues and options in 2020

As already indicated, the future of renting as an option for the baby boom generations in later life is far from clear. Renting, apart from the de-luxe end of the private sector, has become a tenure for those on low incomes. Maclennan, Gibb and More (1990) estimated that almost half of households in social housing in Britain do not now have access to employment income. This is unlikely to change, therefore social and private renting are likely to continue to attract a high proportion of the older baby boomers on low incomes.

What are the main housing problems these older people are likely to experience? Three crucial issues are likely to be availability, affordability and disrepair, because these are at the heart of debates about renting as a tenure in the UK. With regard to the private renter, the aim of recent Conservative governments has been to revitalise this sector by reducing rent restrictions and by opening up access to capital borrowing (eg by lowering interest rates), although there is little evidence that this is having the desired effect (Kemp, 1993). A second plank of government policy has been to replace local authorities with housing associations as the developers of new socially rented housing. The government has also encouraged people on low and middle incomes to consider owner-occupation, not only through the right to buy their council houses but also through policies designed to force rents up in local authority and housing association properties (Malpass and Means, 1993).

Low income households, including those who are older, have been partially protected through the housing benefit system, although the government has been looking at ways of reducing this growing form of public expenditure (Kemp, 1994). Housing associations are expected to generate more and more of their capital investment for new housing from the private market rather than from the government-funded Housing Corporation. The impact of this is not only ever-rising rents (Randolph, 1993) but also a growing reluctance from the private sector to lend money to housing associations, whose debts are becoming high relative to assets (Coles, 1994). A resultant collapse in new building could pose a real challenge to the future availability of socially rented housing for the baby boomers in later life.

Finally, disrepair problems in the rented sector are extensive (Leather, Mackintosh and Rolfe 1994) and show signs of getting worse. Local authorities lack access to funds that would enable them to maintain an ageing housing stock and one in which the 'better' homes have tended to have been bought by their tenants. Disrepair in the housing association sector has traditionally been lower than in council housing, but a dramatic change will occur in the next twenty-five years unless housing associations are able to operate a financial regime in which they can set aside adequate sums for long-term maintenance.

All of this means that people on low and middle incomes in socially rented housing will have to make difficult decisions about whether to stay within their present tenure despite the problems mentioned above or to opt for the equal difficulties associated with owning. In the survey of housing attitudes by Hedges and Clemens (1994) for the Department for the Environment (see earlier discussion), 20 per cent of the 1091 renters had once owned, and 38 per cent of the

Table 7.3 Renters and whether they had previously owned or
considered buying, by age group

	16–34	35–54	55+	Total
Never owned (%)	88	68	83	80
Base no. (all renters)	(330)	(275)	(480)	(1091)
Of those who never owned, percentage who considered buying	43	49	29	38
Base no. (never owned)	(290)	(186)	(397)	(876)

Source: Hedges and Clemens (1994).

873 tenants who had never owned had seriously considered owner-
occupation as an option, including 49 per cent of those in the 35–54
age band (Table 7.3). The fact of the matter is that both owning and
renting are problematic tenures for people on low incomes. Hence, it
is extremely difficult to predict the future drift into and out of renting
in the next twenty-five years.

However, it is possible to argue that, unless there is a major reversal before 2020 of housing policies towards those who rent, insecurity
will be the key housing issue for older baby boomers who rent their
home, and this insecurity will take numerous forms. One aspect will
be insecurity over whether rent levels will be affordable even with
access to housing benefit (Marsh and Riseborough, 1995). Many will
feel insecure about their tenancy rights, especially if they live in the
private sector; in this respect, it should be noted that the Housing Act
1996 further reduces these rights by making all new tenancies on or
after 28 February 1997 open to repossession after six months. Insecurity will be experienced about landlords in terms of their motivations
and even their future viability. With regard to housing associations,
there must be some concern that many of the smaller and medium
sized associations will experience complete financial collapse. For people in council housing, the government has been developing competitive tendering for housing management, which means that housing
associations and private sector organisations as well as 'in house'
teams of housing managers could be responsible for the day to day
housing management of council estates by 2020 (Clapham and
Franklin, 1994). It is impossible to predict whether older tenants will
develop confidence in these new arrangements. Equally, they are

likely to experience growing anxiety about home security and neighbourhood vandalism, as the overall impact of government policy is to assign a residual and marginal role to socially rented housing, and especially to council housing. For ethnic minority elders, this is likely to take the particularly unpleasant form of racial harassment on many occasions.

Finally, older baby boomer tenants are likely to experience great insecurity and uncertainty over whether to stay put in their existing tenancy or to seek a move within the rented sector, and in particular into some form of flat, bungalow or sheltered housing. The logic of Care and Repair and Staying Put schemes is that most people want to avoid having to move in later life and that one reason for this is that 'the home' is the ideal place to reminisce (Commission on Family Housing, 1994). Some research in housing studies argues that only owner-occupiers develop this high level of identity with their homes (Saunders, 1990), although this has been challenged by others (Gurney and Means, 1993; Langan, Means and Rolfe, 1996) who argue that raising of a family in a particular rented home is just as likely to generate the same positive feelings.

Moving into sheltered housing is nevertheless seen as a positive development by many older tenants (Riseborough and Niner, 1994). However, it is equally clear some older tenants in three-bedroomed houses are pressured to consider a move to smaller property and thus release their present home for a homeless family or one on the waiting list. They are seen as under-occupying their present home and hence open to the accusation of selfishness in a way that is rarely if ever applied to those who own family houses. A study for the government by Barelli (1992) found that potential movers were attracted far more to offers of two-bedroomed houses and bungalows than to offers of one-bedroomed or bedsitter accommodation, including sheltered housing. The Housing Corporation (1996) has recently acknowledged the need to consider offering funding support for new two-bedroomed properties for older people if this encourages them to vacate three-bedroomed rented housing. Such pressures are likely to have increased substantially by the time the baby boom generations enter retirement unless there is a substantial reversal of government policies towards rented housing in the next twenty-five years.

Linked to this, it can also be predicted that the next twenty-five years will see a crisis over the future direction of sheltered housing for rent in both the local authority and the housing association sectors (McCaffery, 1994). Overall high levels of tenant satisfaction are still often recorded by surveys of sheltered housing residents. Riseborough and Niner (1994s), in their study of 755 tenants of Anchor Housing Association schemes, found that 91 per cent of respondents expressed satisfaction with their flat.

So what is the crisis faced by such accommodation? First, as identified by Barelli (1992), there is a growing desire by older tenants to have two bedrooms rather than one bedroom let alone bedsitter accommodation. However, the existing sheltered housing stock is dominated by one-bedroomed properties combined with a sizeable bedsitter stock. A survey of the housing stock of one particular district council, where a recent 'special' needs housing study was carried out (Means et al, 1994), found that the bedsitter accommodation was becoming increasingly difficult to let, as were several of the older schemes where there were often shared toilets and bathrooms. A more recent national survey by Tinker, Wright and Zeilig (1995) found that 92 per cent of local authorities and 79 per cent of housing associations had some difficulty in letting sheltered housing. It is highly likely that the problem of 'hard to let' sheltered housing schemes will grow over the next twenty-five years, and that it will be the poorest and most vulnerable elders from the baby boom generations who will be pressured to accept the least popular sheltered accommodation because their housing need is likely to be greatest and bargaining power weakest (Means, 1990; Tinker et al, 1995).

The second challenge faced by sheltered housing relates to the ambiguity over whether it is a form of housing or a form of community care for people with low 'dependency' needs, a debate further confused by the emergence of 'very sheltered' housing schemes as a potential alternative to residential care (McCafferty, 1994; Means and Smith, 1994; Tinker et al, 1994). One 'difficulty' with people with low dependency needs is that these needs are likely to intensify as they become older, with growing pressures on wardens who may feel ill-equipped to cope with the deteriorating health of the residents. The survey by Means et al (1994) suggests that one response to this from housing providers is to encourage entry to residential and nursing home care. Thus, the housing scenario potentially faced by older people in sheltered housing is that some local authorities and some housing associations will treat it as one step on a conveyor belt leading to residential and nursing home care rather than as a home for life except in the most extreme circumstances. On a more positive note, Kitwood, Buckland and Petrie (1995) found that people who develop dementia when in sheltered housing can fare well if wardens are given appropriate support. Some local authorities and housing associations are increasingly seeing 'extra care' housing as a 'home for life' with a pivotal contribution to make to community care.

So what are the rental options that we need to develop to meet the housing needs of older people in 2020? The central thrust has to be a commitment to produce affordable homes to rent for older people on low incomes who do not wish to own. This accommodation must be maintained by private and public sector landlords to a high standard. Without this, many low income older people will experience homelessness, while others will be forced to pay high rents for houses that are in extremely poor repair. One possibility for achieving such aims with regard to council housing would be their transfer to 'arms length' companies who could use the value, or equity, of existing provision to enable them to borrow money from the market for new building and for renovation outside of public sector borrowing limits (Hills, 1993). All landlords need to recognise that the clear preference of older people is for flats, bungalows and houses to which care services can be brought in if and when their health deteriorates.

Rented housing must also take on board the principles of a home that can adapt to one's changing needs throughout life. Thus, improved access and mobility standards are as crucial in new rented accommodation as in new homes for owner-occupation and should be enshrined in building regulations along the lines proposed by the Access Committee of England (Brewerton and Darton, 1997). In addition to this, housing authorities and housing associations need to develop a more sophisticated approach to the upgrading of dwellings so that, for example, the rewiring of properties could be used as an opportunity to raise plugs, lower switches etc (Means et al, 1994). Recent research by Bonnett (1996) confirmed that it is possible to

incorporate lifetime home standards into modernisation and refur-
bishment programmes for socially rented housing. Over time, this
would reduce the number of requests for specialist adaptation and the
need for older tenants to move into sheltered housing. The third
dimension of a 'home for life' strategy in the rented sector involves a
commitment to support older tenants in sheltered housing in their
own homes when their health deteriorates, through appropriate
health and social care packages. Social services authorities and housing authorities should cease to support the development of new sheltered housing schemes by housing associations not committed to a
home for life.

▪ Conclusion

This brings us back to the whole issue of sheltered housing for rent
and its future role in housing provision for the baby boomers. New
models of sheltered housing are required based on a smaller number
of units built to higher space standards (ie larger) and with less
emphasis on the common lounge. Wardens could then become
responsible for a number of schemes. More generally there is a need
for :

> Models of care . . . to provide maximum flexibility. Consideration should
> be given to moving away from fixed patterns of care to selected very shel-
> tered housing schemes to more flexible patterns of care which can be
> delivered to any tenant in any sheltered scheme who needs a very shel-
> tered setting. This will maximise the potential of all sheltered housing to
> maintain vulnerable elderly people in the community and out of institu-
> tional care. (Fletcher, 1991)

Progress along these lines in the next twenty-five years must be
paralleled by a hard-headed review of all existing sheltered housing
schemes to identify those whose useful life has or is about to come to
an end. These schemes need to be either updated (eg introduction of
lifts to second floor flats), re-remodelled for a new client group, or
demolished and the site developed. Unless this happens, the slum
housing for older people in 2020 will be 'hard to let' sheltered housing
schemes.

Even with these changes, most older people in rented accommodation will not be in sheltered housing, and will not wish to enter such accommodation as their health deteriorates. It is, therefore, crucial that government remains committed to home adaptation in the rented sector through the disabled facilities grant. Housing authorities need particular help in this area. They either have to draw on the disabled facilities grant for which they receive no exchequer support when the adaptation is to their own property or from their own hard-pressed housing revenue account or capital programme (Heywood, 1994). As a result, housing authorities are often hostile to requests from occupational therapists for home adaptations, especially if the older tenant is living in a three-bedroomed house. The best way forward would seem to be an extension of exchequer subsidy combined with local authorities developing a high quality data base of their adapted properties so that adaptation can be seen as a long-term investment in meeting the housing needs of disabled people (Disabled Persons Accommodation Agency, 1995).

Finally, housing authorities and housing associations need to make much greater use of information technology for their tenants, and indeed to provide services for those in owner-occupation. The most obvious example of this would be a further expansion of community alarm systems. Such systems can be criticised if they start from the ageist assumption that all older people need to be protected from risk. However, they do have the potential to help older people in a number of situations, including medical emergencies, help when immobilised, urgent requests for personal assistance and concerns about personal security (Thornton and Mountain, 1992). This chapter started with an emphasis on one's home as a place of security, privacy and independence. It is perhaps fitting to conclude with an emphasis on the capacity of community alarms in the future to reassure people about their personal safety within their own home and hence to contribute to the ability of people to 'stay put' despite increased frailty when that is their choice.

▪ Summary

- The three main housing problems likely to face older baby boomers are availability, affordability and disrepair.

- They will also need a *home* where they can feel relaxed and secure, surrounded by their personal possessions. Thus, housing options will need to be developed to maximise the ability to make a genuine home in whatever accommodation option is chosen.

- More baby boomers will be owner-occupiers than previous generations of older people.
  - Present debates concerning the ability of older owner-occupiers to repair and maintain their homes may have less resonance for the baby boomers who are at the heart of the DIY movement.
  - More pertinent may be issues of security, loneliness and mobility. As Maria Evandrou discusses in Chapter 8, the solutions to these may lie in increased use of information technology – with community alarm systems, home shopping and 'drop-in' centres via the Internet, and innovations concerning the use of aids and adaptations in the home.
  - Better options for equity release will also be required.

- Social and private renting will continue as major housing tenures into the twenty-first century and will attract a high proportion of older baby boomers on low incomes.
  - The decline in new building in this sector, combined with growing disrepair problems, may result in a lack of appropriate housing for the baby boomers in later life.
  - Unless there is a reversal of policy, older renters will face growing insecurity on a number of fronts: will rents remain affordable?; will there be continuing entitlement to housing benefit?; what will happen to tenancy rights?
  - Landlords need to recognise the preference of older people for two-bedded properties that can be adapted to changing needs throughout life.

8 Building a future retirement: towards a policy agenda

Maria Evandrou

As we have seen in the preceding chapters, tomorrow's ageing baby boomers will differ from today's older people in a number of important respects, reflecting the fact that they were born and grew up in very different economic, technological and social climates. It is useful to summarise briefly some of the major findings and projections and draw out their implications for the baby boomers in retirement.

The world that the baby boomers will inhabit in 2020 and beyond will be different from that experienced by today's older people in a number of fundamental ways. The baby boomers will have different expectations of their retirement and of the welfare state. Most notably, technology will affect the daily work, family and social life of individuals and families. The likely effects of technological innovation on the lives of the baby boomers in retirement – both as a means of empowerment and as a mechanism acting to reinforce existing trends towards greater polarisation – are examined. The chapter then discusses key issues that any future policy agenda should address, and the need for long-term planning is emphasised. To what extent these concerns are taken on board will ultimately depend on political will and the extent to which the baby boomers exercise their electoral strength.

■ What future for the baby boomers in retirement?

Little attention has been paid to the likely socio-economic characteristics of the baby boom generations in the first few decades of the

twenty-first century, and how they may differ from previous generations of older people. The baby boomers have experienced patterns of
family life, work, housing and health that are different from those of
today's older people. The implications of these trends and experiences
for the baby boomers in retirement, both in terms of their needs for
income support, health and social care and in their quality of life in
old age, are outlined below.

Demographic trends

Demographic trends, outlined by Jane Falkingham in Chapter 1, will
influence the potential availability of personal care in old age from
spouses and children for the baby boomers in retirement. Most of the
first baby boomers married, and married young. During the 1980s
there was a shift towards later marriage, and it is likely that a greater
proportion of the second baby boomers will never have married or
formed a serious cohabiting union, than have preceding cohorts. Some
may be in serious relationships, just not cohabiting. At the same time,
the incidence of divorce has been increasing and a greater proportion
of both baby boomers are likely to have experienced the break-up of a
union by the time they reach retirement than have today's older people. This has implications both for the level of resources in later life,
especially for women and their income from an ex-husband's pension,
and for the availability of informal social care.

In addition to rising divorce, the birth rate has been going down
since 1964. More of second baby boomers are likely to be childless
than the first baby boomers, and those who do have a family are likely
to have fewer children. Demographic trends will also influence the
household composition of the older baby boomers. Greater proportions of 75-year-olds in the first baby boom cohort will be 'living solo'
than have previous cohorts and it is likely that this proportion will be
even greater among the second baby boomers. As argued in Chapter
6, there will be fewer potential sources of informal support to rely on
when the baby boomers age. Those who have the financial resources
will be in a position to purchase the social support necessary to
remain in their own home for as long as possible. This may include
aspects of 'smart housing' technology that facilitate independent

living (discussed further below). However, the outlook for childless second boomers on a low income may well be bleak, their being forced to rely on whatever services will be provided by the state and voluntary sectors.

Health

The extent to which the baby boomers will be in need of health and social care will reflect levels of ill-health and dependency. A review of the trends by Gillian Dalley in Chapter 4 concluded that the evidence on the future health of the boomers is mixed. Trends in smoking provide one indication that the baby boomers may be healthier in later life than today's older people. However, the proportion reporting limiting long-standing illness suggests the opposite, younger cohorts reporting slightly *higher* levels than previous cohorts at the same age. Furthermore, the second baby boom has experienced higher levels of unemployment, and longer working weeks for those in work, earlier in their life course has than the first boom cohort. Increased levels of work-related stress may manifest themselves in poorer health in older ages. Some evidence for increased stress and feelings of dislocation from society among the second baby boomers is provided by the rise in suicide rates among them today, particularly men (Charlton, 1996; Kelly, 1995). Whether the baby boomers will be healthier than today's older people may also depend on the impact of factors as yet unknown. We will have to wait to see whether the greater use of pesticides, genetic engineering in animal farming and advances in food technology will manifest themselves in better or worse health in later life (Bone et al, 1995).

Employment and resources

Chris Phillipson, in Chapter 2, discussed how industrial change since World War 2 has resulted in the emergence of alternative working practices, reflected in the growth of part-time working and self-employment. For some this has brought with it greater flexibility, allowing people to combine multiple responsibilities such as child care, elder care and paid employment. For others it has resulted in a lack of long-term security and fewer employment-related benefits such as occupational pensions, maternity leave and holiday entitlements. The 'traditional' life course with defined periods of education, work and retirement is being replaced by one in which there is significantly more fluidity and movement between states, especially in the labour market. The notion of a *lifelong* career has all but disappeared. Rather, temporary and transitional jobs will become a permanent feature of the employment experiences of some of the second baby boomers.

Changes in the labour market have affected men and women differently. In Chapter 3, Ruth Hancock showed that younger generations of men both enter the labour market later and leave earlier and have *lower* overall participation rates at any given age. In contrast, women from the second baby boom experience *higher* rates of participation at any given age (and higher full-time rather part-time employment), than earlier generations. Both of these trends have implications for the level of resources in later life. More women have longer working lives, spending more time in full-time employment (if often at lower pay than men), enhancing their potential for accumulating pension entitlement in their own right. The shorter working lives of men, however, will tend to have the opposite impact, reducing overall pension entitlements.

There has been an increase in membership of occupational pension schemes over time within the cohorts, especially among women. Fewer of second baby boom men are members of occupational pensions schemes than previous generations, but both men and women of the second baby boom are more likely to have personal pensions. For the younger baby boomers at least, the usual certainty of occupational pensions, with a defined benefit (pension payments based on a proportion of final salary), has been transformed into the uncertainty of private pensions, in which the final pay-out depends on the 'lottery of the money markets' (Atkinson, 1991).

More of the baby boomers than previous generations will have access to housing wealth, both through their own tenure and through inheritance. Between three-quarters and four-fifths of the first baby boom cohort, and an even greater proportion of the second boomers, will enter retirement owning their own homes .

Both rising membership of pension schemes and greater levels of owner-occupation point to the baby boomers being better off in retirement than are today's pensioners. However, any complacency concerning the retirement incomes of the boomers is premature. Inequalities will persist between those who will have experienced full work histories, acquired pension rights and housing wealth, and those who have not. Furthermore, among those who retire with housing equity, some may be faced with selling their home later on to finance their long-term care needs (Harding, Meredith and Wistow, 1996).

Widening inequalities and increasing polarisation

A central theme highlighted throughout the book is the likelihood of increasing polarisation within the boomers. The second baby boom cohort, in particular, faced high levels of unemployment when they began to enter the labour market. Some of this group have never had a full-time job and, thus, the opportunity to accumulate resources and participate actively in society. The recession of the 1980s also hit the first baby boomers. Many of those who lost their jobs in their mid-40s faced particular difficulties in re-entering the labour market during a period of technological change. Early retirement for this group has often been not through choice but circumstance. Interrupted work histories will perpetuate into old age the inequalities stemming from unemployment and low income.

Differences in inheritance of housing wealth will further reinforce the trend towards polarisation. Holmans and Frosztega (1994) found that a greater proportion of local authority tenant couples than owner-occupier couples, do *not* have owner-occupiers as parents on either side, lending support to the contention that inheritances of house property will go in the most part to individuals who are themselves owner-occupiers and already able to accumulate wealth. Handing on wealth from one generation to the next reinforces to notion that the rich get richer while the poor remain the same – further contributing to 'two nations in retirement' (Titmuss, 1955).

Polarisation in terms of financial resources will also lead to inequalities in access to health and social care through changes in the ways that the health and social care services are financed. Private health insurance has risen in the last decade, and some companies are offering social insurance policies. People with uneven employment histories are unlikely to be in a position to contribute to either private pensions or private health insurance. Yet, given that employment in turn is related to health status, these groups may be in most need of health care.

We are already witnessing the explicit rationing of publicly funded health care, free at the point of use (Maynard, 1993; New and Le Grand, 1996; Grimley Evans, 1997; Williams, 1997). As Gillian Dalley discussed in Chapter 4, age discrimination already seems to be operating in relation to a variety of treatments and care (Whitaker, 1992; Seymour, 1993); in times of greater pressures on financial resources, this is likely to continue to grow. Cases such as the one that occurred in Hillingdon Hospital – where in October 1996 it was announced that, owing to a lack of available beds, all people aged 75 and over referred by their GP for emergency treatment would be refused – may become more widespread (Hunt, 1996). Other examples of rationing health care for particular age groups include no physiotherapy for those aged 65-plus in a hospital in a south-eastern coastal town. If the current trends towards a two-tier health service continue, by 2020 the poorly resourced older people who are unable to purchase services outside the NHS may find themselves dependent on a residualised publicly funded service in which exclusion from particular treatments, on the grounds of age, is commonplace.

Charging for social care services has become more widespread. The Department of Health expected that, on average, one-tenth of the cost of direct service provision in 1996/7 would be met through charges to users (Neate, 1996). By 2020 it is likely that local authorities will be required to raise charges so that they can recover a greater proportion of the full economic cost of the services they offer. People who are uninsured and with low or no private pension income are unlikely to be able to meet such charges themselves, and will be faced with either a means-tested service or a service they cannot afford.

Thus, baby boomers at the bottom of the income distribution may find themselves multiply disadvantaged: without the resources to participate in society, without the income to exercise choice over formal and informal sources of social care and possibly excluded from particular medical treatment.

■ The role of technology in 2020 and beyond

So far we have focused on the hurdles and difficulties that might face particular groups among the ageing baby boomers, from a 1990s economic and social policy perspective. Before we turn towards the policy agenda, however, it is important to recognise that technological innovation will mean that the world in 2020 will offer different options. Technology has permeated all spheres of our lives and will continue to change the face of daily living in the twenty-first century, both through innovation in consumer durables and other goods and through enhanced communication and access to information. The key question is how these developments will affect the quality of life and well-being of older baby boomers in the next century.

Computers and the rapidly expanding use of the Internet are revolutionising the exchange of information. It is not unrealistic to envisage that in the future most homes, or at the very least every public library or advice centre, will have access to the information superhighway via the Internet. Already hospital trusts are 'publishing' in electronic form waiting lists for different specialties and by 2020 it will be the norm for every social services department to have their own 'home page' and consumers will have immediate access to information concerning what services are available, at what price and by which agency.

Information technology may also facilitate greater participation among older people themselves: for example, using the network offers opportunities to access debates and policy discussions as well providing feedback to trusts and other organisations about the quality of services used. Physical incapacity will no longer be a barrier to accessing such technology through the use of voice- or sensory-activated computers. Access to the Internet via the TV will bring virtual meeting rooms, art galleries, museums and even holidays in exotic locations directly into your own living room. Interactive cable networks will offer a wide use of public services, advice lines, transactions from home, entertainment and library services, home security, service metering and itemised billing, facilitating the everyday life activities of everyone in the next century. Technology can thus empower people as citizens and consumers.

Technological innovation may also enhance the independence and quality of daily living of older people. As well as providing access to information, new products will facilitate the lives of people with disabilities through 'smart' technology. For example, trials are already being conducted of community alarms in which sensors in an older person's home, locally processed via computer networks, can help to identify unusual behaviour, such as the person becoming unconscious or having a fall (Sixsmith and Sharples, 1996). This then triggers the alarm for help. Smart technology will provide greater environmental control, such as hand-held controls to open and close windows or voice-activated systems to boil the kettle. A 'smart house system' could help people in the early stages of dementia to remain within their own home. The key issues in 2020 will not be the availability of such systems but rather their affordability and portability. Will systems be easily transferable when people move home? Will they be sensitive to the dynamic nature of dependence and changing needs?

Another sphere in which technological advances will affect the lives of the ageing baby boomers is medical care. Telemedicine, whereby medical advice or care will be administered in one's own home through a communications link (eg a videophone) will become more commonplace. Such technologies give rise to new implications for the 'rights' of individuals; for example, with telemedicine, the person can switch off the machine and put a halt to any further medical care or advice – a response that is not so easy in a hospital environment where the individual would have little control (Fisk, 1996). Telecommunications may also replace low skill community services such as monitoring people and make existing services more efficient and cost effective. Such community care technologies can enhance people's independence and help older people to remain in the community for longer. Furthermore, with greater opportunities for home working and flexible employment, individuals with multiple responsibilities may be better placed to combine paid work with family care.

'Smart medicine', such as spinal implants that enhance mobility, and medical breakthroughs in areas such as Alzheimer's disease, will have an enormous impact on the quality of life to be expected among baby boomers in 2020. Reports on the isolation of the Alzheimer's gene have raised expectations of a cure in the future. However, just as the infectious diseases of the nineteenth century have been replaced by the degenerative diseases of the twentieth century, so too may the twenty-first century produce its own new diseases. The effects of environmental pollution and synthetic chemicals have yet to be fully determined.

That technological innovation will play a much bigger role in the lives of the ageing baby boomers in the twenty-first century is not contentious in my view. However, that it will *necessarily* enhance their well-being, that it will manifest itself into affordable, portable and transferable gadgets or services is far from self-evident. A critical approach to new technology, and how it affects people's lives, has yet to be developed. Will 'smart housing' and community care technologies be sensitive to race and culture? What about technological overload or the potential for 'over-care'? How do we ensure that design is user-driven rather than technologically pushed? The involvement of a wide range of users, carers and older people more generally in the design of such products and services is essential. Critically, will the benefits of technology be accessible to a wide range of groups or will lack of access to, for example, the Internet be another dimension of inequality? Will the *'connected'* and *'not connected'* be the 'haves' and the 'have nots' of the future? This will depend on the shape of future policy.

■ Shaping future policy

To what extent will the baby boomers shape social policy in the first few decades of the twenty-first century? Their sheer number, composition and expectations are all likely to play a role. Most of the debate to date regarding policy and the baby boom generations has focused on their size. The large post-war birth cohorts approaching retirement age, worsening dependency ratios and greater pressure on the social security and welfare services budgets, has given rise to a flourishing literature on the social and economic costs of an ageing population both in Britain and in North America, much of which has been pessimistic (Johnson, Conrad and Thomson, 1989; Aaron, Bosworth and Burtless, 1989). But rising dependency ratios do not automatically translate into demographic despair (Falkingham, 1989; Henwood, 1993). Not all older baby boomers will be dependent and it is important to recognise that many will make an active contribution both as producers and as consumers. Furthermore, technological innovation may change the relationship between the labour market and economic growth.

As we have seen, differences among the baby boomers may be as great as the differences between age groups. Trends towards greater polarisation among the baby boomer generations will demand a social policy response, unless society is content to allow a growing proportion of the older population to be residualised and 'excluded'. The very size of these groups of baby boomers will make them more visible. They are likely to be more vocal in their demands.

Great expectations?

The baby boomers are better educated than previous generations and have become sophisticated consumers. The notion of retirement is taken for granted and there are clear expectations associated with it. Most see it as a period of leisure in return for a lifetime of work and expect to have a period of active and relatively healthy old age, 'not in work and not in poverty'. Two-thirds of older people today are healthy and live independently without requiring support from family or formal agencies. One-third of informal carers are older themselves. Older people have become the focus of market researchers as private enterprise chases after the 'grey pound'. Increasingly, older people are remaining active in social and economic life, as well as taking up new ventures. Will the older baby boomers in 2020 and beyond assert their lifestyles even more distinctly? Will 'growing old disgracefully' become the catch-phrase for the next century? The new millennium elders who were nurtured on megabytes, microfibre and media imaging are likely to be more discerning consumers both of leisure activities and of health and welfare services.

The baby boomers also have distinct ideas concerning the welfare state and what they can expect from it as a right, especially with regard to health care and pension provision. Here there are differences between the first and second baby boomers, the latter being more sceptical about the continuance of a Beveridge-type state pension when they retire. Nevertheless, people still expect the government to take responsibility for the core areas of welfare provision (Jowell et al, 1994). Social care agencies, purchasing authorities and trusts in 2020 will be faced with clients who will expect to be fully involved in the development of services.

The grey vote: minority or majority interests?

Politicians may have to take on board the views and demands of the baby boomers, as, electorally, they will constitute a significant minority to be reckoned with. In 1991 the total potential electorate in Great Britain constituted 44.7 million people aged 18 years and over, of whom nearly a quarter (10.6 million) were aged 60–65-plus. By 2021, the size of this latter age group will have risen to over 17 million, increasing the share of the 'grey vote' from a quarter (23.7 per cent) to one third (33.7 per cent). Given that older people are far more likely than younger people to be registered to vote, this proportion will probably be even greater. Furthermore, policies that relate to ageing issues are also the interests and concerns of individuals in middle-age. People aged 45 and over will constitute over half of those eligible to vote in 2021. Some may argue that it is too simplistic to assume that people will vote according to the age group they represent. However, age-based politics has already progressed much further in the USA, groups such as the Gray Panthers and America for Generational Equity constituting powerful lobby groups (Johnson and Falkingham, 1992). Single-issue voting has also taken on greater importance in the late twentieth century and may take centre stage in the next. The use of technology may help people to become more informed about political and policy issues at home, as well as voting via the Internet from their living room. Electoral turnout would take on a very different meaning.

■ Planning ahead: towards a policy agenda

The sheer size of the baby boom cohorts will necessitate some change in policy formulation and implementation locally. But whether this will be the result of a series of responses and incrementalism, rather than the outcome of explicit and coherent longer-term policy planning, remains to be seen.

Planning ahead for the retirement of the baby boomers requires a long-term view. Nowhere is this more applicable than in the case of income in retirement and pension provision. Changes in the rules of pension schemes today will affect the likely returns tomorrow. However, long-term planning does not fit well within the five-year electoral cycle and difficult decisions about the future costs of the ageing baby boomers are all too easily set aside in favour of short-term political gain. Indeed an advisor to Ronald Reagan in the late 1980s questioned why any government of the day would be prepared to 'mortgage their political reputation for tomorrow's agenda'. But it could also be argued that it is in everyone's interests that government *does* begin to plan to ensure that structures are in place to minimise the numbers affected by poverty, social exclusion and inadequate service development.

Issues for policy

Future public policy will need to take on board a number of issues.

Widening inequalities and increasing polarisation Many of the baby boomers will be 'well resourced' in old age and able to purchase health and social care services outside the public sector. But there will be a significant minority who will not have accumulated resources across their working life. In the 1990s generally the poor have got poorer while the rich have become richer (Joseph Rowntree Foundation, 1995). This may have longer-term implications, in particular for the second baby boomers.

The gap between the resourced and under-resourced is likely to be wider in 2020 and beyond: those of the second baby boomers who were in work reaped the benefits of higher wages and lower taxes while those who experienced unemployment, endured longer periods of it and diminishing state provision. Widening inequalities will characterise the differences between the two boomer cohorts.

Providing for ethnic diversity The ageing of black and minority ethnic communities has so far received very little attention. Progress by the social services agencies in the provision of appropriate support services for a multicultural society has been slow and uneven. In part this is due to the relatively small numbers of minority ethnic elders today. However, one in fourteen of the second baby boomers is from a minority ethnic group. Adequate provision for a multi-racial population in 2020 will be critically important.

Combating ageist practices Future planning needs to learn from current experiences in which financial pressures have resulted in policies that reinforce ageist practices. This contradicts principles of equity and the underpinning philosophy of the NHS of 'equal treatment for equal need'. Such practices may also be politically unwise in 2020 when the grey vote will carry greater weight.

Facilitating greater user involvement and advocacy The involvement of clients and users for the design and development of appropriate and flexible services is gaining greater currency. The rights of users and citizens will take on greater importance, especially the role of advocacy, as the boomers assert their demands in old age.

Valuing older boomers as a resource It has been argued that in the twenty-first century Britain may face a skills shortage as the number of younger workers diminishes. This ignores that fact that the older boomers will constitute a reservoir of knowledge and skills that can be drawn on. They will also offer an additional source of labour, in both the formal and the informal sectors.

Policy agenda

Bearing the above issues in mind, any future policy agenda should address the following.

Income and social security Alleviating poverty will be central in social security planning. The extent to which any safety net is part of a universal system of benefits based on citizenship or a targeted system based on need will in large part depend on the commitment of future governments. If current trends towards a residualised welfare state continue, the challenge for future social security policy will be to ensure some minimum standard of living in retirement for *all* baby boomers, avoiding the worst aspects of means-testing – such as stigma and low take-up – and heightened social exclusion. Social policy should reflect experience *over* the life course (Evandrou and Falkingham, 1995). Future policies should aim to:

- maximise the individual's potential through positive employment and training policies;
- provide a safety net that minimises stigma.

Health and social care With the ageing of the baby boomers, will the cost of health care for older people be out of control and unsustainable? Analysts argue that there is no evidence that Britain cannot afford the NHS (Hills, 1993; Wardsworth, Donaldson and Scott, 1996; Harrison et al, 1997). Neither is there any evidence to suggest that in 2020 or 2040 we will not be able to afford a welfare state. It will be important to ensure that the eligibility criteria for collectively provided care do not become so narrowly defined that baby boomers who cannot pay for social care themselves, and who are unable or unwilling to rely on family care, increasingly risk falling through the safety net. Future policies should aim to:

- provide a choice of flexible, appropriate and responsive services tailored to their needs;
- improve preventative services, health promotion and screening, especially among particular groups such as ethnic elders.

Employment Employment policies should:

- encourage the retention of older workers – the abolition of age thresholds on training schemes would encourage older workers who wish to remain in, or re-enter, the labour market to enhance their skills;
- facilitate training both of younger successors by older workers and of older workers themselves;
- incorporate planning for phased and flexible retirement;
- be flexible, offering family-friendly practices to allow for multiple responsibilities.

Mechanism

So that the baby boomers can plan for their retirement with some degree of certainty, there must be some stability in certain areas of social policy such as pensions. If rules are subject to frequent changes no one can be certain what their pension contributions will entitle them to. Although promises are often made, the history of pension scheme provision over the past century has been one of exaggerated claims and disappointed expectation (Johnson and Falkingham, 1994). It can be argued that there is a need for part of the planning structure to be outside the five-year electoral cycle – removed from the traditional political arena.

At present there is little or no coherent strategy recognising the links between income support, housing, health and social care. Changes in one sector (eg the introduction of a charge for a service that was previously supplied free of charge) will affect another sector (recipients of benefit will require a higher income to maintain the same standard of living). Lack of integrated planning can give rise to the emergence of perverse incentives, such as those created by changes in the social security rules regarding housing support and payments for nursing homes in 1980, which resulted in local authorities relying on DHSS payments to support older people in private residential care rather than provide such care themselves within the local authority (Evandrou, Falkingham and Glennerster, 1990).

One solution for this is to establish an Ageing Commission or to include ageing within the remit of the Equal Opportunities Commission, to make available the forum for debate, information gathering and investigating different policy options, and by which winners and losers of different policy strategies are evaluated and made explicit. An alternative is to have a Minister responsible for ageing. In the USA there is an Assistant Secretary for Aging within the Department of Health and Human Services. Part of their brief includes specific responsibilities for the planning for the ageing of the baby boomers in the USA.

■ Baby boomers: our future in our hands?

Long-term planning requires debate at all levels. Without it the elder boomers could 'end up' with a residual welfare state by default – merely providing a minimal safety net for the most deprived. George and Miller (1994) advocate

> giving the public the choice between a residual welfare state with low taxes and a citizen's welfare state at a higher tax cost before the former wins out by default on the assumption that it is the only way of squaring the welfare circle.

Baby boomers themselves need to realise their own potential in shaping their future retirement prospects, ensuring that issues are debated, different options evaluated and long-term planning embarked on where required. As we have seen, they will constitute a significant proportion of the electorate. If they choose to exercise their electoral muscle with one voice, no future government would be wise to ignore them.

REFERENCES

INTRODUCTION

Evandrou M, Falkingham J (1997) *Growing Old in Twenty-first Century Britain: The experience of four cohorts 1974–1993*, Welfare State Programme Discussion Paper No 128. London School of Economics, London.

Goodman A, Webb S (1994) *For Richer, For Poorer: The changing distribution of income in the UK, 1961–91*, IFS commentary No 42. Institute for Fiscal Studies, London.

Johnson P, Falkingham J (1992) *Ageing and Economic Welfare*. Sage, London.

OECD (1988) *Ageing Populations: The social policy implications: Demographic change and public policy*. OECD, Paris.

OPCS (1995) *1992-based National Population Projections*, Series PP2 No 19. HMSO, London.

1 WHO ARE THE BABY BOOMERS?

Allen I, Hogg D, Peace S (1992) *Elderly People: Choice, participation and satisfaction*. Policy Studies Institute, London.

Babb P, Bethune A (1995) 'Trends in births outside marriage', *Population Trends*, 81, Autumn: 17–22.

Clarke L (1992) 'Children's family circumstances: recent trends in Great Britain', *European Journal of Population*, 8: 309–340.

Coleman D (1996) 'New patterns and trends in European fertility', in D Coleman (ed) *Europe's Population in the 1990s*. Oxford University Press, Oxford, 1–61.

CSO (1996) *Social Trends 1996*. HMSO, London.

Douglas J W B (1970) 'Broken families and child behaviour', *Journal of the Royal College of Physicians*, 4: 203–10.

Evandrou M (1992) 'Challenging invisibility of carers: mapping informal care nationally', in F Laczko and C R Victor (eds) *Social Policy and Elderly People: The role of community care*. Avebury, Aldershot, 1–29.

Evandrou M, Falkingham J (1995) 'Gender, lone-parenthood and lifetime incomes', in J Falkingham and J Hills (eds) *The Dynamic of Welfare*. Prentice Hall/Harvester Wheatsheaf, London, 167–183.

Evandrou M, Falkingham J (1997) *Growing Old in Twenty-first Century Britain: The experience of four cohorts 1974–1993*, Welfare State Programme Discussion Paper No 128. London School of Economics, London.

Falkingham J (1989) 'Dependency and ageing in Britain: a re-examination of the evidence', *Journal of Social Policy*, 18/2: 211–233.

Ferri E (1984) *Stepchildren: A national study*. NFER-Nelson, London.

Grundy E, Harrop A (1991) 'Co-residence between adult children and their elderly parents in England and Wales', *Journal of Social Policy*, 21/3, 325–348.

Haskey J (1993a) 'First marriage, divorce and remarriage: birth cohort analyses', *Population Trends*, 72, Summer: 24–33.

Haskey J (1993b) 'Trends in the number of one-parent families in Great Britain', *Population Trends*, 71, Spring: 26–33.

Haskey J. (1994a) 'Estimated numbers of one-parent families and their prevalence in Great Britain in 1991', *Population Trends*, 78, Winter: 5–19.

Haskey J (1994b) 'Stepfamilies and stepchildren in Great Britain', *Population Trends*, 76, Summer: 17–28.

Haskey J (1995) 'Trends in marriage and cohabitation: the decline in marriage and the changing pattern of living in partnerships', *Population Trends*, 80, Summer: 5–15.

Johnson P, Falkingham J (1992) *Ageing and Economic Welfare*. Sage, London.

Kiernan K (1992) 'The impact of family disruption in childhood on transitions made in young adult life', *Population Studies*, 46: 213–234.

Kiernan K, Eldridge S (1985) *A Demographic Analysis of First Marriages in England and Wales: 1950–1980*, Centre for Population Studies Research Paper 85-1. CPS/London School of Hygiene and Tropical Medicine, London.

Kiernan K, Wicks M (1990) *Family Change and Future Policy*. Joseph Rowntree Memorial Trust/FPSC, York.

Millar J (1994) 'Lone parents and Social Security policy in the UK', in S Baldwin and J Falkingham (eds) *Social Security and Social Change: New challenges to the Beveridge model*. Harvester Wheatsheaf, London, 62–76.

Murphy M (1993) 'Time-series approaches to the analysis of fertility change', in M Ni Bhrolchain (ed) *New Perspectives on Fertility in Britain*, Studies on Medical and Population Subjects No 55. HMSO, London, 51–66.

OPCS (1995a) *1992-based National Population Projections*, Series PP2 No 19. HMSO, London.

OPCS (1995b) *Marriage and Divorce Statistics*, Series FM2 No 21. HMSO, London.

OPCS (1995c) *Birth Statistics*, Series FM1 No 22. HMSO, London.

OPCS (1996) *Living in Britain: Results from the 1994 General Household Survey*. HMSO, London.

2 Employment and training:
planning for 2020 and beyond

Atkinson A B, Sutherland H (1993) 'Two nations in early retirement? the case of Britain', in A B Atkinson and M Rein (eds) *Age, Work and Social Security*. Macmillan, London.

Blackwell J (1992) 'Labour market participation and retirement of older workers', in *OECD Employment Outlook*. OECD, Paris.

Bone M, Gregory J, Gill B, Lader D (1992) *Retirement and Retirement Plans*. OPCS Social Survey Division, London.

Buck N, Gershuny J, Rose D, Scott J (1994) *Changing Households: The British Household Panel Survey 1990–1992*. ESRC Research Centre for Micro-Social Change, University of Essex, Colchester.

Burrows R, Loader B (eds) (1994) *Towards a Post-Fordist Welfare State?* Routledge, London.

Coopers and Lybrand (1992) *People's Training and Development – the vision and the reality*. Coopers and Lybrand, London.

Corti L, Laurie H, Dex S (1994) *Caring and Employment*, Employment Department Research Series No 39. Employment Department, London.

Doeringer P (ed) (1990) *Bridges to Retirement*. Cornell University / ILR Press, Ithaca NY.

Ellison R (1994) 'British labour force projections: 1994–2006', *Employment Gazette*, 102(4): 111–122.

Ellison R, Butcher S, Melville D (1995) 'British labour force projections: 1995–2006', *Employment Gazette*, 103(4): 153–168.

Employment Department Group (1994) *Getting On: The benefits of an older workforce*. EDG, London.

Health Education Authority (1994) *Investing in Older Work*. HEA, London.

Hewitt P (1993) *About Time: The revolution in work and family life*. Rivers Oram Press, London.

Institute of Personnel Management (1993) *Statement on Age and Employment*. IPM, London.

Itzin C, Phillipson C (1993) *Age Barriers at Work*. METRA, Solihull.

Kohli M, Rein M, Guillemard A-M, Gunsteren H (1991) *Time for Retirement: Comparative studies of early exit from the labour force*. Cambridge University Press, Cambridge.

Laczko F, Phillipson C (1991) *Changing Work and Retirement*. Open University Press, Milton Keynes.

Lange T, Atkinson J (1995) *Employment Trends and Prospects for Older Workers to 2030*. Institute for Employment Studies, University of Sussex, Brighton.

McGoldrick A, Arrowsmith J (1993) 'Recruitment advertising: discrimination on the basis of age' *Employee Relations*, 15(5): 54–65.

Metropolitan Authorities Recruitment Agency (1994) *Lifting The Age Barrier*. METRA, Solihull.

Moody H (1993) 'Overview. What is critical gerontology and why is it important?', in T Cole, W A Achenbaum, P Jakobi, R Kastenbaum (eds) *Voices and Visions of Aging*. Springer Publishing, New York.

Moore J, Tilson B, Whitting G (1994) *An International Overview of Employment Policies and Practices Towards Older Workers*, Research Series No 29. Employment Department, London.

Naylor P (1990) *Age No Barrier*. Metropolitan Authorities Recruitment Agency, Solihull.

O'Reilly J, Caro F (1994) 'Productive aging: an overview of the literature', *Journal of Aging and Social Policy*, 6(3): 39–71.

Phillips J (ed) (1995) *Working Carers and Older People*. Avebury, Aldershot.

Phillipson C, Strang P (1983) *The Impact of Pre-Retirement Education*. University of Keele, Department of Adult Education, Stoke-on-Trent.

Phillipson C (1993) 'The sociology of retirement', in J Bond, P Coleman, S Peace (eds) *Ageing and Society: An introduction to social gerontology.* Sage, London.

Re-Action Trust (1992) *Is Retirement Working?* Re-Action Trust, London.

Taylor P, Walker A (1993) *Age and Employment: Policies, attitudes and practice.* IPM, London.

Taylor P, Walker A (1994) 'The ageing workforce: employers' attitudes towards older people', *Work, Employment and Society,* 8(4): 569–591.

Trinder C, Hulme G, McCarthy U (1992) *Employment: The role of work in the third age.* Public Finance Foundation, London.

Watson G (1994) 'The flexible workforce and patterns of working hours in the UK', *Employment Gazette,* July: 239–248.

Witherspoon S, Taylor B (1990) *British Social Attitudes 1989 Survey: A report for the Employment Department.* Social and Community Planning Research, London.

3 FINANCIAL RESOURCES IN LATER LIFE

Askham J, Hancock R, Hills J (1995) *Opinions on Pensions: Older people's attitudes to incomes, taxes and benefits.* Age Concern Institute of Gerontology, King's College, London.

Atkinson A B (1994) *State Pensions for Today and Tomorrow.* Age Concern Institute of Gerontology, King's College London, London.

Atkinson A B (1995) *The Welfare State and Economic Performance,* Welfare State Programme discussion paper No WSP/109. STICERD/London School of Economics, London.

Barr N (1992) 'Economic theory and the Welfare State: a survey and interpretation', *Journal of Economic Literature,* [XXX], June: 741–803.

Barr N (1993) *The Economics of the Welfare State,* 2nd edn. Oxford University Press, Oxford.

Beveridge W (1942) *Social Insurance and Allied Services: Report by Sir William Beveridge,* Cmnd 6404. HMSO, London.

Bone M, Gregory J, Gill B, Lader D (1992) *Retirement and Retirement Plans*. HMSO, London.

Castle B, Townsend P (1996) *We* can *afford the Welfare State*. Security in Retirement for Everyone, London.

Commission on Social Justice (1994) *Social Justice: Strategies for national renewal*. Institute for Public Policy Research, London.

Dawson A, Evans G (1987) 'Pensioners' incomes and expenditure 1970 to 1985', *Employment Gazette*, 95(5): 243–252.

Department of Social Security (1993) *Equality in State Pension Age*. HMSO, London.

Department of Social Security (1995a) *Social Security Statistics 1995*. HMSO, London.

Department of Social Security (1995b) *The Pensioners' Incomes*, Series 1993. DSS, Analytical Services Division, London.

Department of Social Security (1995c) *Income Related Benefits: Estimates of take-up in 1993/4*. DSS, Analytical Services Division, London.

Department of Social Security (1997) 'Guaranteed, secure pensions for all', says Peter Lilley. DSS Press Release, 5 March.

Dilnot A, Johnson P (1992) 'What pension should the state provide?' *Fiscal Studies*, 13: 4.

Employment Department (1996) 'British labour force projections: 1996–2006', *Labour Market Trends*, May. HMSO, London.

Evandrou M, Falkingham J (1997) *Growing Old in Twenty-first Century Britain: The experience of four cohorts 1974–1993*, Welfare State Programme Discussion Paper No 128. STICERD / London School of Economics, London.

Falkingham J, Johnson P (1993) *A Unified Funded Pension Scheme for Britain*, Welfare State Programme Discussion Paper No WSP / 90, STICERD / London School of Economics, London.

Field F, Owen M (1993) *Private Pensions for All: Squaring the circle.* Fabian Society, London.

Gibbs I, Oldman C (1993). *Housing Wealth in Later Life: a mixed blessing?*, Discussion Paper 5. University of York, Centre for Housing Policy.

Goodman A, Webb S (1994). *For Richer, For Poorer: The changing distribution of income in the UK, 1961–91*, IFS commentary No 42. Institute for Fiscal Studies, London.

Gosling A, Machin S, Meghir Costas (1994) 'What has happened to men's wages since the mid-1960s?', *Fiscal Studies*, 15(4): 63–87.

Government Actuary's Department (1994) *Occupational Pension Schemes 1991: Ninth survey by the Government Actuary.* HMSO, London.

Government Actuary's Department (1995) *National Insurance Fund Long Term Financial Estimates.* HMSO, London.

Hancock R, Jarvis C (1994) *Long Term Effects of Being a Carer.* HMSO, London.

Hancock R, Weir P (1994) *More Ways Than Means: A guide to pensioners' incomes in Great Britain during the 1980s.* Age Concern Institute of Gerontology, London.

Hancock R, Jarvis C, Mueller G (1995) *The Outlook for Incomes in Retirement: Social trends and attitudes.* Age Concern Institute of Gerontology / King's College London, London.

Hansard (1995) 13 February, col 536.

Hills J (1993) *The Future of Welfare: A guide to the debate.* Joseph Rowntree Foundation, York.

Holmans A, Frosztega M (1994) *House Property and Inheritance in the UK.* HMSO, London.

Hutton S, Kennedy S, Whiteford P (1995) *Equalisation of State Pension Ages: The gender impact.* Equal Opportunities Commission, Manchester.

Jarvis C, Hancock R, Askham J, Tinker A (1996) *Getting Around After 60.* HMSO, London.

Johnson P, Disney R, Stears G (1996) *Pensions: 2000 and Beyond*, vol. 2: *Analysis of Trends and Options*. Retirement Income Inquiry, London.

Lynes T (1996) *Our Pensions: A policy for a Labour government*. Eunomia, London.

Mullings B, Hamnett C (1992) 'Equity release schemes and equity extraction by elderly households in Britain', *Ageing and Society*, 12: 413–442.

OPCS (1996) *Living in Britain: Results from the 1994 General Household Survey*. HMSO, London.

Retirement Income Inquiry (1996) *Pensions 2000 and Beyond*, vol 1: *Report of the Retirement Income Inquiry*, chaired by Sir John Anson. Retirement Income Inquiry, London.

Rolfe S, Leather P, Mackintosh S (1993) *Available Options: The constraints facing older people in meeting housing and care needs*. Anchor Housing Trust, Oxford.

Townsend P, Walker A (1995) *The Future of Pensions: Revitalising National Insurance*. Fabian Society, London.

World Bank (1994) *Averting the Old-Age Crisis*. Oxford University Press, Oxford.

4 HEALTH AND HEALTH CARE

Benzeval M, Judge K, Whitehead M (1995) *Tackling Inequalities: An agenda for action*. King's Fund, London.

Blaxter M (1990) *Health and Lifestyles*. Tavistock/Routledge, London.

Carr-Hill R (1987) 'The inequalities in health debate: a critical review of the issues', *Journal of Social Policy*, 16/4: 509–542.

Central Statistical Office (1996) *Social Trends 1996*. HMSO, London.

Chancellor of the Exchequer and the Secretaries of State (1996) *A New Partnership for Care in Old Age*. HMSO, London.

Chew R (1995) *Compendium of Health Statistics*. Office of Health Economics, London.

Culyer A J (1991) 'The promise of a reformed NHS: an economist's angle', *British Medical Journal*, 302/6787: 1253–1256.

Curtice J (1993) 'Satisfying work – if you can get it', in R Jowell et al (eds) *International Social Attitudes: the 10th British Social Attitudes Report*. SCPR, London.

Dalley G (1996) *Ideologies of Caring: Rethinking community and collectivism*, 2nd edn. Macmillan, Basingstoke.

Davies S, Chandler D (1994) *Hypothecated Taxation and the Future of UK Healthcare*. Independent Healthcare Association, London.

Department of Health (1993a) *On the State of the Public Health. The Annual Report of the Chief Medical Officer for the Department of Health for the Year 1992*. HMSO, London.

Department of Health (1993b) *Making London Better*. DoH, London.

Department of Health, Central Monitoring Unit (1992) *The Health of Elderly People: an epidemiological overview*, vol 1. HMSO, London.

Department of Health, Welsh Office and Scottish Office (1996) *Choice and Opportunity: Primary care – the future*. HMSO, London.

Devis T (1990) 'The expectation of life in England and Wales', *Population Trends*, 60, Summer.

Evandrou M, Falkingham J (1997) *Growing Old in Twenty-first Century Britain: the experience of four cohorts 1974–1993*, Welfare State Programme Discussion Paper No 128. STICERD/London School of Economics, London.

Fries J F (1983) The compression of morbidity', *Milbank Memorial Fund Quarterly*, 61: 397–419.

Gregg P, Wadsworth J (1995) 'The short history of labour turnover, job tenure and job security, 1975–1993', *Oxford Review of Economic Policy*, 11/1: 73–90.

Henretta J C (1994) 'Recent trends in retirement', *Reviews in Clinical Gerontology*, 4: 71–81.

Hutton W (1995) 'Why they should want to put down the older generation', *Guardian*, 6 February.

Joseph Rowntree Foundation (1995) *Income and Wealth. Report of the Joseph Rowntree Foundation Inquiry Group*. JRF, York.

McKee I, Laing W (1993) *Rationing Medicine: A review of the implications of limiting the provision of health care resources*. Association of the British Pharmaceutical Industry, London.

McKeown T (1979) *The Role of Medicine: Dream, mirage or nemesis?* Basil Blackwell, Oxford.

Manton K G (1986) 'Past and future life expectancy increases at later ages: their implications for the linkage of chronic morbidity, disability and mortality', *Journal of Gerontology*, 41 / 5: 672–681.

Manton K G (1989) 'Life-style risk factors', *Annals of the American Academy of Political and Social Science*, May: 503.

Marmot M, Shipley M, Rose G (1984) 'Inequalities in death – specific explanations of a general pattern?, *Lancet*, May 5:1003–1006.

Marmot M, Shipley M (1996) 'Do socioeconomic differences persist after retirement? 25-year follow up of civil servants from the first Whitehall study', *British Medical Journal*, 313: 7066.

NHS Executive (1995) 'Purchasing with practice: new developments in purchasing and fundholding', *Purchasing in Practice*, issue 2, February, Performance Management Directorate, NHS Executive.

NHS Management Executive (1993) *New World – New Opportunities: Nursing in primary health care*. HMSO, London.

Secretary of State for Health (1992) *The Health of the Nation: A strategy for health in England*, Cm 1986. HMSO, London.

Seymour D G (1993) 'The aging surgical patient: a selective review of areas of recent clinical and research interest', *Reviews in Clinical Gerontology*, 3: 231–244.

Smaje C (1995) *Health, Race and Ethnicity: Making sense of the evidence.* King's Fund, London.

Smith A, Jacobson B (1988) *The Nation's Health: A strategy for the 1990s.* King's Fund, London.

Social Security Advisory Committee (1994) *State Benefits and Private Provision.* The Review of Social Security paper 2. SSAC, London.

Tallis R (1994) 'Medical advances and the future of old age', in M Marinker (ed) *Controversies in Health Care Policies.* BMJ Publishing Group, London.

Thane P (1989) 'Old age: burden or benefit?' in H Joshi (ed) *The Changing Population of Britain.* Basil Blackwell, Oxford.

Tomlinson Sir Bernard (1992) *Report of the Inquiry into London's Health Service, Medical Education and Research.* HMSO, London.

Touche Ross (1994) *Evaluation of Nurse Practitioner Pilot Projects.* South Thames Regional Health Authority / NHS Executive South Thames, London.

Victor C (1994) *Old Age in Modern Society: A textbook of social gerontology.* Chapman & Hall, London.

Walker A, Guillemard A-M, Alber J (1991) *Social and Economic Policies and Older People.* First Annual Report of the European Observatory. Commission of the European Communities, Brussels.

Walker A R P, Walker B F (1993) 'Nutritional and non-nutritional factors for "healthy" longevity', *Journal of the Royal Society for Health,* April: 75–80.

Whitaker P (1992) 'Rationing, ageism and the new look NHS', *Geriatric Medicine,* 22: 1.

5 COMMUNITY CARE

Allen I, Hogg D, Pearce S (1992) *Elderly People: Choice, participation and satisfaction*. Policy Studies Institute, London.

Association of Metropolitan Authorities (1994) *A Survey of Social Services Charging Policies 1992–4*. AMA, London.

Audit Commission (1986) *Making a Reality of Community Care*. Audit Commission, London.

Audit Commission (1993) *Taking Care: Progress with care in the community*. Audit Commission, London.

Baldock J (1994) 'The personal social services: the politics of care', in V George and S Millar (eds) *Social Policy towards 2000. Squaring the Welfare Circle*. Routledge, London.

Baldock J, Ungerson C (1994) *Becoming Consumers of Community Care*. Joseph Rowntree Foundation, York.

Bebbington A, Davies B (1993) 'Efficient targeting of community care: the case of the home help service', *Journal of Social Policy*, 22(3): 373–391.

Bradshaw J, Gibbs I (1988) *Public Support for Private Residential Care*. Avebury, Aldershot.

Cheetham J (1993) 'Social work and community care in the 1990s: pitfalls and potentials', in R Page and J Baldock (eds) *Social Policy Review*, 5.

Committee of Public Accounts (1988) *Twenty Sixth Report*. HMSO, London.

Davies B, Bebbington A, Charnley H (1990) *Resources, Needs and Outcomes in Community-Based Care*. Avebury, Aldershot.

Deakin N, Wright A (1990) *Consuming Public Services*. Routledge, London.

Department of Health (1990) *Community Care in the Next Decade and Beyond. Policy Guidance*. HMSO, London.

District Audit Service (1992) *Constructing Budgets for Purchasing Community Care.* Audit Commission, London.

Finch J, Groves D (eds) (1983) *A Labour of Love.* Routledge, London.

Harden I (1993) *The Contracting State.* Open University Press, Milton Keynes.

House of Commons Health Committee (1993) *Sixth Report. Community Care: The way forward,* HC 482-I, (482-I). HMSO, London.

Hoyes L, Lart R, Means R, Taylor M (1994) *Community Care in Transition.* Joseph Rowntree Foundation, York.

Lewis J, Meredith B (1988) *Daughters who Care.* Routledge, London.

Lewis J, Glennerster H (1996) *Implementing the New Community Care.* Open University Press, Buckingham.

Means R, Smith R (1985) *The Development of Welfare Services for Elderly People.* Croom Helm, London.

Richards S (1994) 'Making sense of needs assessment', *Research Policy and Planning,* 12(1): 5–9.

Secretary of State for Social Security (1997) *A New Partnership for Care in Old Age,* Cm 3563. HMSO, London.

Sinclair I, Parker R, Leat D, Williams J (1990) *The Kaleidoscope of Care: A review of research on welfare provision for elderly people.* HMSO, London.

Stewart J, Walsh K (1992) 'Change in the management of public services', *Public Administration,* 70(4): 499–518.

Titmuss R M (1968) 'Community care: fact or fiction?' (lecture delivered in 1961) in R M Titmuss, *Commitment to Welfare.* Allen and Unwin, London.

Ungerson C (1987) *Policy is Personal: Sex gender and informal care.* Tavistock, London.

Walker A (1982) 'The meaning and social division of community care', in A Walker (ed) *Community Care: The family, the state, and social policy.* Blackwell and Martin Robertson, Oxford.

Wistow G, Knapp M, Hardy B et al (1994) *Social Care Markets: Progress and prospects*. Open University Press, Milton Keynes.

Wistow G (1995) 'Coming apart at the seams', *Health Services Journal*, 2 March: 24–25.

6 SOCIAL CARE: TODAY AND BEYOND 2020

Arber S, Ginn J (1995) 'Gender differences in informal caring', *Health and Social Care in the Community*, 3: 19–31.

Audit Commission (1996) *Balancing the Care Equation: Progress with community care*, Community Care Bulletin No 3. HMSO, London.

Baxter C (1988) 'Ethnic minority carers: the invisible carers', *Health and Race*, 15: 4–8

Bone M, Bebbington A, Jagger C, Morgan K, Nicolaas G (1995) *Health Expectancy and its Uses*. HMSO, London.

Bowling A (1984) 'Caring for the elderly widowed – the burden on their supporters', *British Journal of Social Work*, 14: 435–455.

Braithwaite V (1990) *Bound to Care*. Allen and Unwin, London.

Cicirelli V (1983) 'A comparison of helping behaviour to elderly parents of adult children with intact and disrupted marriages', *Gerontologist*, 23/6.

Clements L (1996) 'A real act of care', *Community Care*, No 11, 14–20 March: 26–27.

Clifford D (1990) *The Social Costs and Rewards of Caring*. Avebury, Aldershot.

Daatland S (1990) 'What are families for? On family solidarity and preference for help', *Ageing and Society*, 10: 1–15.

Department of Health (1989) *Caring for People*. HMSO, London.

Diba R (1996) *Meeting the Costs of Continuing Care: Public views and perceptions*. Joseph Rowntree Foundation, York.

Dunnell K (1995) 'Population review. 2. Are we healthier?', *Population Trends*, 82, Winter: 12–18.

Evandrou M (1992) 'Challenging the invisibility of carers: mapping informal care nationally', in F Laczko and C Victor (eds) *Social Policy and Older People*. Avebury, Aldershot.

Evandrou M, Winter D (1992) *Informal carers and the labour market in Britain*, Welfare State Programme Discussion Paper No 89. STICERD/LSE, London.

Evandrou M. (1995) 'Paid and unpaid work: the socio-economic position of informal carers in Britain', in J Phillips (ed) *Working Carers and Older People*. Avebury, Aldershot.

Evandrou M, Falkingham J (1995) 'Gender, lone-parenthood and lifetime incomes', in J Falkingham and J Hills (eds) *The Dynamic of Welfare*. Prentice Hall/Harvester Wheatsheaf, London, 167–183.

Evandrou M (1996) 'Unpaid work, carers and health', in D Blane, E Brunner and R G Wilkinson (eds) *Health and Social Organisation: Toward a health policy for the 21st century*. Routledge, London.

Finch J (1995) 'Responsibilities, obligations and commitments', in I Allen and E Perkins (eds) *The Future of Family Care for Older People*. HMSO, London, 51–64.

George L, Gwyther L (1986) 'Caregiver well-being: a multidimensional examination of family caregivers of demented adults', *Gerontologist*, 26(3): 253–259.

Glendinning C (1990) 'Dependency and interdependency: the incomes of informal carers and the impact of Social Security', *Journal of Social Policy*, 19/4: 469–497.

Grant G, Nolan M (1993) 'Informal carers: sources and concomitants of satisfaction', *Health and Social Care*, 1: 147–159.

Grundy E (1992) 'Socio-demographic change', in Department of Health *The Health of Elderly People: An Epidemiological Overview*, Companion Papers. HMSO, London, 1–9.

Jerrome D (1996) 'Ties that bind', in A Walker (ed) *The New Generational Contract*. UCL Press, London, 81–99.

Kendig H (1986) 'Intergenerational exchange', in H Kendig (ed) *Ageing Families: A support networks perspective*. Allen and Unwin, Sydney.

Kendig H, Hashimoto A, Coppard L (1992) *Family Support for the Elderly: The international experience*. Oxford University Press, Oxford.

Knodel J, Napaporn C, Siriboon S (1992) 'The impact of fertility decline on familial support for the elderly: an illustration from Thailand', *Population and Development Review*, 18: 79–103.

McCalman J (1990) *The Forgotten People: Carers in the ethnic minority communities in Southwark*. Kings Fund Centre, London.

Means R, Smith R (1994) *Community Care: Policy and Practice*. Macmillan, London.

Nolan M, Grant G (1992) *Regular Respite: An evaluation of a hospital rota bed scheme for elderly people*, Research Monograph Series. Age Concern Institute of Gerontology / ACE Books, London.

Oldman C (1991) *Paying for Care: Personal sources of funding care*. Joseph Rowntree Foundation, York.

OPCS (1992) *General Household Survey 1990 Report*. HMSO, London.

Parker G (1990) *With Due Care and Attention: A review of research on informal care*, 2nd edn. FPSC, London.

Parker G (1993) *With This Body: Caring and disability in marriage*. Open University Press, Milton Keynes.

Parker G, Lawton D (1994) *Different Types of Care, Different Types of Carer: Evidence from the GHS*. SPRU / HMSO, London.

Qureshi H (1996) 'Obligations and support within families', in A Walker (ed) *The New Generational Contract*. UCL Press, London, 100–119.

Qureshi H, Walker A (1989) *The Caring Relationship: Elderly people and their families*. Macmillan, London.

Robine J, Blanchet M, Dowd J (eds) (1992) *Health Expectancy: First Workshop of the International Health Life Expectancy Network (REVES).* HMSO, London.

Siim B (1990) 'Women and the welfare state', in C Ungerson (ed) *Gender and Caring: Work and welfare in Britain and Scandinavia.* Harvester Wheatsheaf, Hemel Hempstead, 80–109.

Sinclair I, Parker R, Leat D, Williams J (1990) *The Kaleidoscope of Care.* National Institute for Social Work / HMSO, London.

Sixsmith A (1986) 'Independence and home in later life', in C Phillipson, M Bernard and P Strang (eds) *Dependency and Interdependency in Old Age.* Croom Helm, London, 338–347.

Stevenson O (1994) 'Paid and unpaid work: women who care for adult dependants', in J Evetts (ed) *Women and Career: Themes and issues in advanced industrial societies.* Longman, Harlow, 87–99.

Thompson C, West P (1984) 'The public appeal of sheltered housing', *Ageing and Society,* 4: 305–326.

Twigg J, Atkin K with Perring C (1990) *Carers and Services: A review of research.* HMSO, London.

Waerness K (1990) 'Informal and formal care in old age: what is wrong with the new ideology in Scandinavia today?', in C Ungerson (ed) *Gender and Caring: Work and welfare in Britain and Scandinavia.* Harvester Wheatsheaf, Hemel Hempstead.

Warnes T, Ford R (1995) 'Migration and family care', in I Allen and E Perkins (eds) *The Future of Family Care for Older People.* HMSO, London, 65–92.

Wenger C (1992) *Help in Old Age: Facing up to change. A longitudinal network study.* Liverpool University Press, Liverpool.

Wright F (1986) *Left Alone to Care.* Gower, Aldershot.

7 HOUSING OPTIONS IN 2020

Ayrton R et al (1990) *Flexible Tenure*. Joseph Rowntree Foundation, York.

Barelli J (1992) *Underoccupation in Local Authority and Housing Association Housing*. HMSO, London.

Bonnett D (1996) *Incorporating Lifetime Homes Standards into Modernisation Programmes*, JRF Housing Research Findings No 174. Joseph Rowntree Foundation, York.

Brewerton J, Darton D (eds) (1997) *Designing Lifetime Homes*. Joseph Rowntree Foundation, York.

Bull J, Poole L (1989) *Not Rich, Not Poor – A study of housing options for elderly people on middle incomes*. SHAC and Anchor Housing Trust, London and Oxford.

Clapham D, Franklin B (1994) *Housing Management, Community Care and Competitive Tendering: A good practice guide*. Chartered Institute of Housing, Coventry.

Coles A (1994) 'Service the secret as money-go-round grinds to halt', *Inside Housing Supplement*, 16 September: 2–3.

Commission on Family Housing (1994) *Housing of Older People: The Lisbon recommendations*. CFH, Brussels.

Department of the Environment (1988) *English House Condition Survey 1986*. HMSO, London.

Department of the Environment (1993) *English House Condition Survey 1991*. HMSO, London.

Department of the Environment (1995) *The Application of the Building Regulations to Help Disabled People in New Buildings in England and Wales*, Consultation Document. DoE, London.

Disabled Persons Accommodation Agency (1995) *The Way Forward for Kent*. DPAA, Rochester.

Fletcher P (1991) *The Future of Sheltered Housing – Who Cares?* Policy Report. National Federation of Housing Associations, London.

Fletcher P, Herbert G (1996) 'Trapped in care', *Community Care*, 4 January: 19.

Gibbs I (1993) *Financial Resources of Older People and Paying for Care in Later Life*, Social Policy Research Findings No 40. Joseph Rowntree Foundation, York.

Gurney C, Means R (1993) 'The meaning of home in later life', in S Arber and M Evandrou (eds), *Ageing, Independence and the Life Course*. Jessica Kingsley, London, 119–131.

Harrison L, Means R (1990) *Housing: The essential element in community care*. SHAC and Anchor Housing Trust, London and Oxford.

Harrison L, Means R (1993) 'Brokerage in action? Radnor care and repair project', in R Smith et al (eds) *Working Together for Better Community Care*, SAUS Study No 7. School for Advanced Urban Studies, Bristol, 113–137.

Hedges B, Clemens S (1994) *Housing Attitudes Survey*. HMSO, London.

Heywood F (1993) *Hoamchoice: A practical guide to housing option appraisal*. School for Advanced Urban Studies, Bristol.

Heywood F (1994) *Adaptations: Findings ways to say yes*. School for Advanced Urban Studies, Bristol.

Higgins J (1989) 'Defining community care: realities and myths', *Social Policy and Administration*, 23/1: 3–16.

Hills J (1993) *The Future of Welfare: A guide to the debate*. Joseph Rowntree Foundation, York.

Housing Corporation (1996) *Housing for Older People*. Housing Corporation, London.

Hutton W (1994) 'Bad times for the good life', *Guardian*, 2 August: 2–3.

Kemp P (1993) 'Rebuilding the private and rented sector', in P Malpass and R Means (eds) *Implementing Housing Policy*. Open University Press, Milton Keynes, 59–73.

Kemp P (1994) 'Housing allowances and the fiscal crisis of the welfare state', *Housing Studies*, 9/4: 531–542

Kitwood T, Buckland S, Petrie T (1995) *Brighter Futures*. Anchor Publications, Oxford.

Langan J, Means R, Rolfe S (1996) *Maintaining Home and Independence in Later Life: Older people speaking*. Anchor Publications, Oxford.

Laslett P (1989) *A Fresh Map of Life*. Weidenfeld and Nicolson, London.

Leather P, Mackintosh S (1992) *Maintaining Home Ownership: The agency approach*. Longman, Harlow.

Leather P, Mackintosh S, Rolfe S (1994) *Papering over the Cracks*. National Housing Forum, London.

McCafferty P (1994) *Living Independently: A study of the housing needs of elderly and disabled people*. HMSO, London.

Mackintosh S, Leather P (1994) 'Funding and managing the adaptation of owner occupied homes for people with physical disabilities', *Health and Social Care in the Community*, 2/4: 229–240.

Maclennan D (1994) *A Competitive UK Economy: The challenge for housing policy*. Joseph Rowntree Foundation, York.

Maclennan D, Gibb K, More A (1990) *Paying for Britain's Housing*. Joseph Rowntree Foundation, York.

Malpass P, Means R (eds) (1993) *Implementing Housing Policy*. Open University Press, Milton Keynes.

Marsh A, Riseborough M (1995) *Making Ends Meet: Older people, housing association costs and the affordability of rented housing*. National Federation of Housing Associations, London.

Means R (1990) 'Allocating council housing to older people', *Social Policy and Administration*, 24/1: 52–64.

Means R, Smith R (1994) *Community Care: Policy and practice.* Macmillan, Basingstoke.

Means R, Streich L, Brown I et al (1994) *Towards Partnership? 'Special' housing needs and policy responses in Woodspring,* Working Paper No 123. School for Advanced Urban Studies, Bristol.

Miller K (1994) 'Sheltered owners at the mercy of the sharks', *Inside Housing,* 26 August: 8–9.

Oldman C (1990) *Moving in Old Age: New directions in housing policies.* HMSO, London.

Randolph B (1993) 'The re-privatisation of housing associations', in P Malpass and R Means (eds) *Implementing Housing Policy.* Open University Press, Milton Keynes, 39–58.

Riseborough M, Niner P (1994) *I Didn't Know You Cared! A survey of Anchor's sheltered housing tenants.* Anchor Housing Trust, Oxford.

Rolfe S, Leather P, Mackintosh S (1993) *Available Options.* Anchor Housing Trust, Oxford.

Rolfe S, Mackintosh S, Leather P (1993) *Age File '93.* Anchor Housing Trust, Oxford.

Saunders P (1990) *A Nation of Home Owners.* Unwin Hyman, London.

Thornton P, Mountain G (1992) *A Positive Response: Developing community alarm services for older people.* Community Care and Joseph Rowntree Foundation, London and York.

Tinker A, McCreadie C, Wright F, Salvage A (1994) *The Care of Frail Elderly People in the United Kingdom.* HMSO, London.

Tinker A, Wright F, Zeilig H (1995) *Difficult to Let Sheltered Housing.* HMSO, London.

Townsend P (1963) *The Family Life of Old People.* Penguin, Harmondsworth.

Webb S, Wilcox S (1991) *Time for Mortgage Benefits.* Joseph Rowntree Foundation, York.

8 BUILDING A FUTURE RETIREMENT: TOWARDS A POLICY AGENDA

Aaron H, Bosworth B, Burtless G (1989) *Can America Afford to Grow Old?: Paying for social security*. The Brookings Institute, Washington DC.

Atkinson A B (1991) 'The development of state pensions in the United Kingdom', in W Schmahl (ed) *The Future of Basic and Supplementary Pension Schemes in the European Community in 1992 and Beyond*. Nomos Verlagsgesellschaft, Baden-Baden.

Bone M, Bebbington A, Jagger C, Morgan K, Nicolaas G (1995) *Health Expectancy and Its Uses*, HMSO, London.

Charlton J, Kelly S, Dunnell K, Evans B, Jenkins R (1993) 'Suicide deaths in England and Wales: trends in factors associated with suicide deaths', *Population Trends*, 71, Spring: 34–42.

Evandrou M, Falkingham J, Glennerster H (1990) 'The personal social services: everyone's poor relative but nobody's baby', in J Hills (ed) *The State of Welfare: The Welfare State in Britain Since 1974*. Oxford University Press, Oxford, 206–273.

Evandrou M, Falkingham J (1995) 'Gender, lone-parenthood and lifetime incomes', in J Falkingham and J Hills (eds) *The Dynamic of Welfare*. Prentice Hall/Harvester Wheatsheaf, London, 167–183.

Falkingham J (1989) 'Dependency and ageing in Britain: a re-examination of the evidence', *Journal of Social Policy*, 18/2: 211–233.

Fisk M J (1996) 'Elderly People and Independent Living: The implications of smart house technologies', paper presented at the British Society of Gerontology Annual Conference, University of Liverpool, 20–22 September.

George V, Miller S (1994) *Social Policy Towards 2000: Squaring the welfare circle*. Routledge, London.

Grimley Evans J (1997) 'Rationing healthcare by age: the case against', *British Medical Journal*, 314: 11–13.

Harding T, Meredith B, Wistow G (eds) (1996) *Options for Long Term Care*. HMSO, London.

Harrison A, Dixon J, New B, Judge K (1997) 'Funding the NHS: is the NHS sustainable?', *British Medical Journal*, 314: 296–298.

Henwood M (1993) 'An agenda for change', in D Hobman (ed) *Uniting Generations*. Age Concern England, London.

Hills J (1993) *The Future of Welfare*. Joseph Rowntree Foundation, York.

Holmans A, Frosztega M (1994) *House Property and Inheritance in the UK*. HMSO, London.

Hunt L (1996) 'Hospital puts ban on elderly patients', *Independent*, 15 October.

Johnson P, Conrad C, Thomson D (eds) (1989) *Workers Versus Pensioners: Intergenerational justice in an ageing world*. Manchester University Press, Manchester.

Johnson P, Falkingham J (1992) *Ageing and Economic Welfare*. Sage, London.

Johnson P, Falkingham J (1994) 'Is there a future for the Beveridge pension scheme?', in S Baldwin and J Falkingham (eds) *Social Security and Social Change: New challenges to the Beveridge model*. Harvester Wheatsheaf, Hemel Hempstead, 255–270.

Joseph Rowntree Foundation (1995) *Inquiry into Income and Wealth*, volume 1. Joseph Rowntree Foundation, York.

Jowell R, Curtice J, Brook L, Ahrendt D (1994) *British Social Attitudes Survey*. SCPR/Dartmouth, Aldershot.

Kelly S, Charlton J, Jenkins R (1995) 'Suicide deaths in England and Wales 1982–92: the contribution of occupation and geography', *Population Trends*, 80, Summer: 16–25.

Maynard A (1993) 'Intergenerational solidarity in health care: principles and practice', in D Hobman (ed) *Uniting Generations*. Age Concern England, London.

Neate P (1996) 'Strapped for cash', *Community Care*, 1–7 August.

New B, Le Grand J (1996) *Rationing in the NHS: Principles and pragmatism*. King's Fund, London.

Seymour D G (1993) 'The aging surgical patient: a selective review of areas of recent clinical and research interest', *Reviews in Clinical Gerontology*, 3: 231–244.

Sixsmith A, Sharples P (1996) 'Community Care Technologies: User needs research on the intelligent community alarm', paper presented at the British Society of Gerontology Annual Conference, University of Liverpool, 20–22 September.

Titmuss R M (1955) 'Pension systems and population change', *Political Quarterly*, 16: 152–166.

Wardsworth S, Donaldson C, Scott A (1996) *Can We Afford the NHS?* IPPR, London.

Whitaker P (1992) 'Rationing, ageism and the new look NHS', *Geriatric Medicine*, 22: 1.

Williams A (1997) 'Rationing health care by age: the case for', *British Medical Journal*, 314: 8–10.

GLOSSARY

A term in **bold** type within a definition indicates
that there is an entry for that term in the Glossary.

Age-specific birth rate is defined as the total number of births to
women in a particular age group (usually taken to be a five-year age
group such as women aged 20–24, 25–29 etc) divided by the total
number of women in that age group.

Average income is taken to refer to *mean* income, ie average income
calculated by summing income across all individuals (or households),
and then dividing by the total number of individuals (or households).
This should be distinguished from **median income**, which is defined
as the value of income for the individual (or household) who is exactly
in the middle of the income distribution. Put another way, 50 per cent
of individuals (or households) have an income *below* the median value
and the other 50 per cent of individuals (or households) have an
income *above* the median value.

Baby boom is a popular term referring to a significant increase in the
annual number of births taking place in a population, sustained for
a number of years. It is commonly applied to the surge in births that
occurred in much of Europe, Australasia and North America following
the end of World War 2. A sharp decline in births following a baby
boom is often referred to as a **baby bust**.

Baby boom cohorts in Britain There are two baby boom cohorts
in Britain. The first is comprised of people who were born during the
peak birth years of 1946–50 immediately following the end of World
War 2. The second baby boom cohort is represented by those born
between 1961 and 1965.

Baby bust *see* under **Baby boom**

Birth cohort *see* **Cohort**

Cohort refers to a group of individuals who share common characteristics or who experienced a significant life event within a given period of time. The most common use of the term is with reference to a *birth cohort* – a group of individuals born during a specified period of time, normally one calendar year or a number of years. For example, the 1946–50 birth cohort refers to all individuals born during the years from 1946 to 1950. Other uses of the term include *marriage cohort* (people who married in the same year) and *educational cohort* (people who completed a certain level of education during the same year).

Cohort analysis is a method for investigating the changes in patterns of behaviour or attitudes of a particular group of individuals – usually those who are linked by year of birth. It follows the progress of a particular **cohort** over time as they pass through different age groups.

Collectively provided care refers to care services that are financed by general tax revenues (ie paid for *collectively* by all tax-payers). Such care services may be provided by central or local government or by other contracted agencies.

Community is a term used to refer either to people living in the same geographic area or to a group of people linked by a common culture, social relationship or other sense of identity.

Community care is the provision of services to dependent people living outside of large residential institutions, usually in their own homes. Such services can be provided by a variety of agents, including local authorities, voluntary organisations and **informal carers**.

Complementarity refers to a complementary relationship, when two goods or services go together. For example, meals-on-wheels can complement the services of a local authority home help. *See also* **Substitutability**.

Cross-sectional survey data refers to information collected from individuals at one particular point in time; eg in 1997. This is in contrast to *longitudinal data,* which refers to data collected from the same individuals at different points in time; eg in 1995, 1996 *and* 1997.

Crude birth rate is defined as the total number of live births in a specified period (usually one calendar year) divided by the total population in that period (usually taken to be the mid-year population). The birth rate is the simplest and commonest measure of fertility. It is, however, affected by the age-structure of the population and particularly by the relative number of women of childbearing age in that population. A better measure to compare levels of fertility between different countries or between different time periods in the same country is provided by the **total period fertility rate**.

Data set is a structured set of information (ie data) held in a computer.

Dependency ratio is the ratio of the economically dependent population to the productive population. Dependency ratios are normally calculated on the basis of age rather than actual economic activity, leading to the use of the term *age dependency ratio.* The ages chosen to represent the number of people who are economically active are largely arbitrary, but the most commonly used age group is 16–64. Here the dependency ratio is defined as the number of people aged below 16 or above 64 divided by the number of people aged 16–64. The overall ratio is sometimes split into its two constituent parts – the *child dependency ratio* and the *old-age dependency ratio.*

Economic activity rate is calculated as the percentage of the population in a given age group that is in the labour force. This should be distinguished from the *employment* rate, which is the percentage of the population in a given age group actually in paid employment. The difference between the two arises because the *labour force* includes both employed people and all those who are unemployed regardless of whether they are in receipt of benefit.

Economically inactive population refers to everyone who is not in the labour force, ie students, people who are retired, keeping house, permanently disabled or otherwise unable to work. It does not include unemployed people.

Efficiency in this context refers to carrying out a task in the least costly way whilst still achieving the intended outcome.

Empowerment means giving people the power to make decisions for themselves. This can be achieved by giving them control over resources, so that they can purchase their preferred service mix for themselves, and by increasing knowledge, so that they can make informed choices.

Equality can have several dimensions: equality of opportunity to achieve desired goals; equality of outcome or result; and equality of condition. It is *equality of opportunity* that is generally meant when referring to equality in education, whilst it is *equality of outcome* that is meant when referring to equality in health or social care (ie equal treatment for equal need).

Equity *see* **Housing equity**

Equity release mechanism is a way of providing an income stream from capital assets. Examples of such mechanisms include a **home income plan** or **rolled-up interest loan**.

Family Expenditure Survey (FES) is a continuous survey of about 900 households per year (or 20,000 individuals). All adults in the household are interviewed. Respondents are asked to keep a detailed diary of all their expenditure over a two-week period. The survey contains detailed information on expenditure and income from a variety of sources plus some limited information on other socio-economic characteristics such as housing and education. The survey is based on a **cross-sectional** sample.

General Household Survey (GHS) is a continuous survey of about 12,000 households per year (or 26,000 individuals). All adults and children in the household are interviewed, obtaining a wide range of information, including health, housing, employment and education. Periodically there is a specialist elderly persons section with specific questions on activities of daily living and service use. The survey is based on a **cross-sectional** sample.

Generation technically is a structural term derived from the parent–child relationship. It is also, however, commonly used to identify a group of individuals who are linked by age or some other experience (*see* **Cohort**).

Gross Domestic Product (GDP) the total value of goods produced and services provided in a country in one year. If total net income from abroad is added to GDP this gives the *Gross National Product (GNP)* – an indication of the total income of the country.

Heterogeneity refers to the degree of diversity of content or experience.

Home income plan refers to the raising of a mortgage on one's home by the homeowner, to purchase an annuity that gives regular income until the death of the homeowner. This regular income is used to pay the mortgage interest and provide an income. No capital repayments are made on the mortgage, which has to be paid off in full when the property is sold, usually on the owner's death. These may also be called *mortgage annuity schemes*.

Home Responsibility Protection is a scheme for people who have caring responsibilities either for children or for dependent adults. It is aimed at protecting individuals' basic pension rights. Under the scheme, claimants receive credits for National Insurance contributions, which in turn count towards 'qualifying years' for the state retirement pension and give eligibility for sickness benefit.

Home shopping refers to the ability to obtain information and purchase goods and services from one's own home without having to physically travel to the shops. In the past, home shopping was confined to catalogues, but now there are a growing number of 'home shopping' channels on the television, through which goods can be ordered over the telephone. The next decade will see increasing use of the Internet. Tesco already has a facility whereby goods can be ordered and paid for over the Internet and either collected or delivered to the person's front door. The range of goods and services covered by home shopping is already being extended to cover financial services such as insurance and pensions.

Housing equity refers to the value of a property after the deduction of any outstanding mortgage and/or charges.

Hypothecated tax is a tax that is levied for a particular purpose, eg a 5 per cent education tax that goes in its entirety to education or a 2 per cent defence tax that is spent entirely on defence. At present, there are no hypothecated taxes in Britain. Even National Insurance contributions, which are perceived by the public as going towards financing pensions, in reality are used to finance a variety of benefits and services. Hypothecated taxes allow tax payers to know exactly how much tax is being raised for what purpose.

ILO Unemployed refers to an International Labour Organisation (ILO) recommended measure used in surveys to define the number of people who are unemployed. It differs from the number of people who are receiving unemployment benefit, as it counts as unemployed everyone aged 16 and over who is without a job, is available to start work in the next 2 weeks and has been looking for a job in the last 4 weeks or is waiting to take up a job already obtained.

Individualism refers to a collection of ideas that stress the importance of the individual in relation to other entities. It is often argued that the modern world has become more individualistic than before, with a greater stress on the individual than on the **community**.

Informal carer is someone who cares for another person, but who is not employed to do so and who is not a member of a voluntary organisation. Informal carers are most commonly the spouse or parent of the dependent person, but they may also be other relatives, friends or neighbours. Generally, informal carers are divided into two groups: those who live with the dependent person (ie *co-resident informal carers*) and those who do not.

Labour demand refers to the set of factors that influence the number of jobs in the economy. Such factors include the growth rate of the economy, the industrial base and technology as well as the wage rate.

Labour force *see* **Economic activity rates**

Labour market participation rates is synonymous with **Economic activity rates** (*which see*).

Labour market rigidity refers to factors that inhibit the free operation of the labour market. Theoretically, in a market without obstacles, wages and salaries will be determined by the demand for and supply of labour. If the demand for workers in one area is greater than the supply of workers, wages will be high. These higher wages will in turn attract workers into the area, thus increasing supply and eventually bringing wages back into line with other areas. Factors that prevent workers moving between jobs in different occupations and areas thus cause rigidity within the labour market.

Labour supply refers to the set of factors that influence the number of people who are available for, and willing to, work in the economy. Such factors include the size of the population of working age, their skill levels and education as well as the wage rate.

Life course refers to the series of changes that take place as people move through the course of their lives; such as biological and social changes, eg childhood, adolescence, adulthood, marriage, parenting, bereavement and old age.

Life expectancy is the average number of years a person would live if current levels of mortality applied throughout their lifetime. The most commonly used measure is life expectancy at birth.

Longitudinal data *see* in **Cross-sectional** data

Market principles operate when goods and services are offered for sale in a market in which the prices for those goods and services are determined by the laws of supply and demand.

Median income *see* in **Average income**

Mortgage annuity schemes *see* **Home income plan**

Multivariate analysis refers to statistical techniques that are used to investigate the relationship between more than two different variables. Such techniques include multiple correlation, regression and cluster analysis. These techniques allow the investigator to look at the relationship between a dependent variable (eg health) and a range of independent variables (eg age, gender, occupation, education), controlling for the effect of each independent variable in turn.

NHS trusts are agencies within the health service that provide services for purchase. These agencies include hospitals, community services and ambulance services.

Old age dependency ratio *see* in **Dependency ratio**

Out-migration is movement of a person or people from one part of the country to another part of the same country. It is often used to refer to movement from rural areas to cities or vice versa. Out-migration should be distinguished from *emigration*, which refers to migration to a foreign country.

Polarisation of society refers to the trend towards society being divided into two groups with opposing economic and social experiences. This is reflected in the growing gap between the haves (eg the work- and income-rich) and the have nots (eg the work- and income-poor).

Population of working age is generally taken to be the population of men aged 16–64 years and women aged 16–59 years, the difference between men and women being due to the differential age of statutory retirement in Britain.

Post-modern is a sociological term that is used to describe economic and social changes in the late twentieth century.

Quintile refers to a segment of the population when that population is divided into five equal groups according to their ranking on a particular variable. For example, if people are ranked by income and then divided into quintiles, the bottom quintile refers to those in the poorest fifth (or 20 per cent) of the income distribution and the top quintile refers to those people in the richest fifth of the income distribution.

Real income is income adjusted for changes in prices over time. Trends in real income therefore show trends in the purchasing power of income over time (*see also* **Real terms**).

Real terms If something (eg income, wages or prices) is expressed in *real terms*, this means that the change in its value over time has been adjusted for changes in prices, ie inflation. For example, if the money value of income has increased by 10 per cent over a year, but prices have risen by 8 per cent, the quantity of goods and services that can be purchased will have increased by only 2 per cent.

Residual welfare state refers to a welfare state that makes only the minimum provision at a minimum level. For example, eligibility for all benefits would be means-tested rather than as of right.

Rolled-up interest loans are raised against the security of the home on which neither interest nor capital repayments are made. Interest accrued on the loan is *rolled-up* and added to the capital. The full amount of capital and 'rolled-up' interest is repaid on the death of the owner or sale of the property. These may also be called *reverse mortgages*.

Safety net refers to the **residual welfare** services and benefits for people on low incomes or without income, who would not otherwise be able to provide for themselves.

SERPS is the acronym abbreviation of the State Earnings Related Pension Scheme. This provides a second tier pension for anyone who is not a member of an occupational pension scheme or private pension plan.

Social housing refers to rented housing where the landlord does not seek to make a profit and is usually in receipt of some form of public subsidy; eg local authority housing or housing association housing.

Social transfer payments refer to grants or other payments not made in return for a productive service; eg unemployment benefit, housing benefit.

Substitutability refers to a situation in which one good or service can act or serve in place of another. For example, informal care may substitute for the services of a local authority home help. *See also* **Complementarity**.

Targeting *see* in **Universality**

Tenure profile refers to the present balance between different types of housing; eg how many people currently own their own home, how many currently rent from the local authority/housing association sector, and how many from the private sector.

Tenure projection is an attempt to predict what types of housing will be used in the future; eg the number of people who will own their own homes, or rent from local authorities or housing associations, or rent from the private sector.

Total period fertility rate measures the average number of children a woman would have if she were to experience the current age-specific fertility rates throughout her child-bearing years. *See also* entry for **age-specific birth rate**.

Transparency is a term used in relation to social security systems to refer to the degree to which the rules, eligibility criteria and subsequent levels of benefit can be easily understood by non-experts. Transparency is widely regarded as a desirable characteristic for any pension scheme, but, given the complexity of most systems, this objective is rarely achieved.

Universality refers to the distribution of benefits or services to everyone in a broad category. An example of a *universal benefit* is child benefit: every child under 16 is entitled to the benefit regardless of the level of their parent's income. The converse of universality is *targeting*, which involves the distribution of benefits or services only to those who meet some criteria of eligibility, usually involving a financial means test. Income Support is an example of a *targeted benefit*.

Warehousing is a term used to indicate providing services and care in bulk.

Workforce refers to the people in employment *plus* the **ILO unemployed**.

Workforce in employment is a measure of people in employment (obtained from employer-based surveys), self-employed, all HM Forces, and participants on work-related government-supported training programmes.

ABOUT AGE CONCERN

Baby Boomers: Ageing in the 21st century is one of a wide range of publications produced by Age Concern England, the National Council on Ageing. Age Concern England is actively engaged in training, information provision, fundraising and campaigning for retired people and those who work with them, and also in the provision of products and services such as insurance for older people.

A network of over 1,400 local Age Concern groups, with the support of around 250,000 volunteers, aims to improve the quality of life for older people and develop services appropriate to local needs and resources. These include advice and information, day care, visiting services, transport schemes, clubs, and specialist facilities for older people who are physically and mentally frail.

Age Concern England is a registered charity dependent on public support for the continuation and development of its work.

Age Concern England
1268 London Road
London SW16 4ER
Tel: 0181-679 8000

Age Concern Scotland
113 Rose Street
Edinburgh EH2 3DT
Tel: 0131-220 3345

Age Concern Cymru
4th Floor
1 Cathedral Road
Cardiff CF1 9SD
Tel: 01222 371566

Age Concern Northern Ireland
6 Lower Crescent
Belfast BT7 1NR
Tel: 01232 245729

▪ Professional, policy & research

Financing Long-Term Care: The crucial debate
William Laing
A major shift of resources will be needed over the coming decades to fund the rapidly growing demand for long-term care. In *Financing Long-Term Care*, the author sets the subject in its demographic and social context, and presents the fundamental policy issues and options that need to be addressed.
£14.95   0–86242–123–3

The Law and Vulnerable Elderly People
Edited by Sally Greengross
This report raises fundamental questions about the way society views and treats older people. The proposals put forward seek to enhance the self-determination and autonomy of vulnerable old people and people while ensuring that those who are physically or mentally frail are better protected in the future.
£7.99   0–86242–050–4

Age: The unrecognised discrimination
Edited by Evelyn McEwen
Comprising a series of discursive essays by leading specialists on evidence of age discrimination in British society today, including the fields of employment, health care, leisure and the voluntary sector, this book is an important contribution to the growing debate.
£10.99   0–86242–094–6

The Community Care Handbook: The reformed system explained
Barbara Meredith
Written by one of the country's leading experts, the new edition of this hugely successful handbook provides a comprehensive overview of the first two years of implementation of the community care reforms and examines how the system has evolved. This second edition is essential reading for all those keen to keep up to date and fully informed on the ever-changing community care picture.

£13.99   0–86242–171–3

If you would like to order any of these titles, please write to the address below, enclosing a cheque or money order for the appropriate amount and made payable to Age Concern England. Credit card orders may be made on 0181-679 8000.

Mail Order Unit
Age Concern England
1268 London Road
London SW16 4ER

Factsheets from Age Concern

Covering many areas of concern to older people, Age Concern's factsheets are comprehensive and totally up to date. There are more than 30 factsheets and each one provides straightforward information and impartial advice in a simple and easy-to-use format. Single copies are available free on receipt of a 9″ × 6″ sae.

Age Concern offers a factsheet subscription service that presents all the factsheets in a folder, together with regular updates throughout the year. The first year's subscription currently costs £40; an annual renewal thereafter is £20.

For further information, or to order factsheets, write to:

Information and Services Division
Age Concern England
1268 London Road
London SW16 4ER

INDEX